Sea Power and the Law of the Sea

Sea Power and the Law of the Sea

Mark W. Janis
Harvard Law School

Studies in Marine Affairs

Lexington Books
D.C. Heath and Company
Lexington, Massachusetts
Toronto

Library of Congress Cataloging in Publication Data

Janis, Mark W
  Sea power and the law of the sea.

  Includes index.
  1.   Maritime law. 2.   Freedom of the seas. 3.   Sea power. I.   Title.
JX4410.J25   341.44'8   76-11973
ISBN 0-669-00717-X

Copyright © 1976 by D.C. Heath and Company.

Published simultaneously in Canada

Printed in the United States of America

International Standard Book Number: 0-669-00717-X

Library of Congress Catalog Card Number: 76-11973

Dedicated to three institutions for the study of navies and the oceans:
The Naval Postgraduate School — Monterey
The Naval War College — Newport
The Royal Naval College — Greenwich

Contents

Foreword   ix

Acknowledgments   xi

Introduction: Navies and the Law of the Sea   xiii

Chapter 1   The United States   1

             United States Naval Interests
               in Law of the Sea Issues   1
             The Role of Naval Interests in the
               United States Ocean Policy Process   10
             The Reflection of Naval Interests in
               United States Ocean Policy   13

Chapter 2   The Soviet Union   23

             Soviet Naval Interests in Law of
               the Sea Issues   23
             The Role of Naval Interests in the
               Soviet Ocean Policy Process   28
             The Reflection of Naval Interests in
               Soviet Ocean Policy   30

Chapter 3   Great Britain   39

             British Naval Interests in Law of
               the Sea Issues   39
             The Role of Naval Interests in the
               British Ocean Policy Process   43
             The Reflection of Naval Interests in
               British Ocean Policy   46

Chapter 4   France   53

             French Naval Interests in Law of
               the Sea Issues   53
             The Role of Naval Interests in the
               French Ocean Policy Process   57
             The Reflection of Naval Interests in
               French Ocean Policy   58

viii

Chapter 5   **Coastal Navy States**   63

Passage through Straits   64

Transit along Coasts   68

Military Use of the Seabed   70

Chapter 6   **Navies and the Development of the Law
of the Sea**   75

Sea Power and the Development of
   Customary Law of the Sea   76
Naval Interests and the Law of the
   Sea Negotiations   80

Chapter 7   **Navies and the New Ocean Order**   89

Naval Interests and National
   Ocean Policies   89
Navies and International Legal
   Developments   91

Index   93

About the Author   101

Foreword

The purpose of the Lexington Books Series on Marine Affairs is to bring significant contributions in marine affairs and policy to the marine community. The series consists of monographs on important contemporary problems and combines high quality with the fast production which is so essential in a rapidly changing field.

I am delighted to have *Sea Power and the Law of the Sea* by Mark Janis for the series. When the law of the sea debate intensified nearly a decade ago, naval/strategic concerns played a prominent role in both the formulation and analysis of national marine policies. During the 1970s most academic work has concentrated on resource-related aspects of policy largely ignoring the role of naval power. This makes Janis' work especially timely since it analyzes the role sea power is going to play as a new legal order crystallizes. Noteworthy in this excellent study is the comparative perspective Janis provides examining naval postures in four leading states: the U.S.A., the Soviet Union, Britain and France. This produces an explicit organizational framework lacking in most other works on the subject. *Sea Power and the Law of the Sea* will make an important contribution to the understanding of sea power as the ocean regime moves from the discussion to the implementation phase.

John King Gamble, Jr.
May 18, 1976
Kingston, Rhode Island

Acknowledgments

Many have helped me prepare this book, but no one else, of course, is in any way responsible for the information and conclusions I present. Although I was a faculty member of the Naval Postgraduate School while a reserve naval officer and a Research Associate of the Center for Advanced Research at the Naval War College, the reader must not assume that the views expressed here are in any way expressive of or sanctioned by the United States Navy. This is a very independent analysis, and it differs in significant ways from official United States naval policy.

My special thanks go to: Vice Admiral Stansfield Turner, USN, and Vice Admiral Julien J. LeBourgeois, USN, presidents of the Naval War College; Professor James King and Commander W. R. Pettyjohn, USN, of the Center for Advanced Research at the Naval War College; Professor Donald C. F. Daniel and Professor Boyd Huff of the Naval Postgraduate School; Professor W. T. Mallison of the Naval War College and George Washington University; Dr. Robert L. Friedheim of the Center for Naval Analyses; Elisabeth Mann Borgese of the Center for the Study of Democratic Institutions; Steven J. Burton of the Legal Advisor's Office of the Department of State; Professor Louis B. Sohn of the Harvard Law School; Professor John King Gamble, Jr., of the Law of the Sea Institute; Captain George La Rocque, USN, United States Naval Attaché to France; Lieutenant Commander Thomas F. Marfiak, USN, formerly a student at the Institut d'Études Politiques de Paris; Captain J. R. Hill, RN, now British Naval Attaché to the Netherlands; Professor B. McL. Ranft of the Royal Naval College, Greenwich; Elizabeth Young of the Fabian Society; P. W. D. Hatt of the Ministry of Defence; Evan Luard, M.P.; Ambassador James Cable of the Foreign and Commonwealth Office; Captain W. E. B. Godsal, RN, formerly with the British Navy Staff Washington; and Lieutenant Commander William Bowman, RN, formerly with the Environmental Prediction Research Facility at the Naval Postgraduate School.

Some seven libraries have been invaluable in my investigations, and I wish to thank their staffs for their assistance: Naval War College Library; Naval Postgraduate School Library; Stanford Law Library; Harvard Law Library; Bodleian Law Library,

Oxford; Royal Naval College Library, Greenwich; and Bibliothèque de l'Institut d'Études Politiques de Paris.

Finally, I would like to thank the editors of the *San Diego Law Review*. Some of the material herein about United States, Soviet, British, and French naval interests in law of the sea issues appeared in my article, "Naval Missions and the Law of the Sea," *San Diego Law Review* 13 (March 1976):583–593, and has been reprinted with their permission.

Introduction: Navies and the Law of the Sea

The law of the sea is in the midst of turmoil. Those who use the oceans to fish, ship, drill for oil and gas, mine, and swim and sail are all affected by the new developments in ocean order. But no maritime actors are more concerned with changes in the law of the sea than are the world's major navies. Traditionally, the easy mobility of naval vessels in international waters has been one of the most potent assets of a powerful navy. Restrictions on the freedoms of the high seas could well transform the nature of naval mobility and the strategy of sea power. A general introduction to sea power, the law of the sea, and their relationship, as well as to the course of this book, is in order here.

Sea power is force and threat of force on the oceans. It is usually embodied in a national navy composed of vessels most of which are armed and capable of striking at other ocean craft and at targets on land. Modern navies sail massive aircraft carriers and tiny patrol boats. There are nuclear-powered submarines that can launch intercontinental ballistic missiles capable of destroying cities and destroyers with depth charges capable of destroying submarines. There are cruisers with many guns and missiles and vessels with little or no armament, such as amphibious craft and research ships.

Nearly every country on a coast, lake, or river has a navy. There are more than 120 navies in all. Most navies can do little more than operate close to home because their vessels are small and rely on local ports for supplies and on the support of land-based guns and aircraft. Some navies can operate far from their own shores. These "blue water" navies have larger ships, which can sustain continued operations in distant waters, and they carry with them sufficient force to do without protection from their coasts. Only four countries have a considerable blue water navy: the United States, the Soviet Union, Great Britain, and France. These are also the four states that have the SSBN, a nuclear submarine armed with intercontinental ballistic missiles.

Unlike armies that are always on the territory of some state, naval forces, especially blue water navies, often operate on international waters which belong to no country. During the 19th century, British sea power, then supreme, helped consolidate an international maritime regime based on the freedoms of the high seas, freedoms to travel and to fish without coastal state regulation outside a 3-mile territorial sea. This was a customary legal regime, not written in any convention or treaty. It was, however, remarkably effective, respected by most states in times of peace from the end of the Napoleonic Wars in 1815 to the end of World War II in 1945. As a result, for over a century, navies and other users of the oceans could sail freely on seas covering some 70 percent of the earth's surface. Only within a narrow band of 3 miles, the territorial sea, did coastal states put some legal limits on the mobility of naval forces.

A quest for economic resources upset this traditional ocean order so favorable for naval mobility. In 1945, the Truman Proclamation asserted United States ownership of the oil and gas beneath the offshore continental shelf, an underwater plateau extending, in many places, hundreds of miles out to sea. Beginning in 1947, Chile, Ecuador, and Peru claimed 200-mile maritime zones to protect their fishing resources. These and other unilateral claims to national control threatened to diminish international waters and to replace free use of the oceans with coastal state management. States that benefited from freedoms of the high seas rejected some or all the claims to extended national zones. The United States was in the uncomfortable position of having been the initiator of the scramble for larger national zones and then leading the battle against national claims in the Tuna Wars. The opposition of the United States to the 200-mile zone was based not only on a desire to protect national tuna fishermen, but on the belief that other maritime interests, such as the Navy, would be adversely affected by the increased jurisdictions.

Fifteen years before the Truman Proclamation, at the Hague in 1930, there had been an unsuccessful attempt to codify the law of the sea and to put the freedoms of the high seas and the 3-mile territorial sea into conventions. The need to reach explicit international agreements became even greater after the war, and in 1949 the United Nations tasked its International Law Commission, an international panel of jurists, to consider the law of the sea and prepare some draft conventions. On the basis of these drafts, the First United Nations Conference on the Law of the Sea concluded four conventions in Geneva in 1958. The Convention on the Continental Shelf accepted the assertion of coastal state control over continental shelf resources, but taken as a whole, the conventions failed to settle the outstanding disputes among states over coastal rights and freedoms of the high seas. Most importantly, the 1958 Geneva Conference could not agree on a limit to the territorial sea. A Second United Nations Conference on the Law of the Sea was convened in Geneva in 1960 especially to grapple with the territorial sea problem, but it failed by one vote to adopt a joint United States and Canadian proposal for a 6-mile territorial sea coupled with an additional 6-mile contiguous zone to protect fishing, and the states went home without an agreement. As more states made more unilateral claims to the oceans, the United States and the Soviet Union began to consider calling another law of the sea conference to deal with limits to the territorial sea.

Another problem left unsettled by the two Geneva conferences was the limit to national control over the seabed. It was this question that stimulated the present rounds of United Nations law of the sea negotiations. Vast manganese nodule resources had been discovered on the ocean floor. These nodules promised large amounts of valuable minerals to those able to exploit them. Without an international agreement, it was likely that only those states with the most advanced technology would benefit from the exploitation of this new resource. Arvid Pardo, the Ambassador of Malta to the United Nations, delivered a speech to the First Committee of the General Assembly in 1967, calling for an international regime to govern the seabed and to distribute the profits from seabed mining to the neediest countries. Pardo's speech led to the establishment of a United Nations Ad Hoc Seabed Committee in 1968, followed by the Permanent Seabed Committee from 1969 to 1973. These committees laid the groundwork for the Third United Nations Conference on the Law of the Sea, which has held substantive sessions in Caracas in 1974, Geneva in 1975, and New York in 1976.

More than 150 states have participated in these modern attempts to write a new law of the sea. Each state has sought to promote national maritime interests in the hope that any new ocean order would facilitate national ocean uses. One of the most important national ocean interests has been the protection of naval operations. This has been true not only for the four major naval powers, but also for states with weaker coastal navies.

Navies, strong and weak, have missions to accomplish. Formally at least, these naval duties are established by the branch of the national government responsible for national security. Naval missions differ greatly both within a navy and among various navies. Some typical missions are coastal defense, protection of shipping and fishermen, nuclear deterrence, amphibious assault, coastal bombardment, and naval presence. Nations and their navies seek to use their sea power in different fashions, depending on perceived national security interests.

As the text illustrates, the law of the sea can aid or impede the use of sea power. Accordingly, navies prefer that certain legal rules be adopted in the law of the sea negotiations, rules which would best facilitate naval operations. Naval interests in the law of the sea are promoted in two forums. First, naval preferences are advanced within national ocean policy processes. As the state attempts to formulate a consistent and cohesive ocean policy, naval interests must sometimes clash with those of other maritime actors, such as fishing, commerce, and oil and gas. Second, insofar as the national policy finally reflects naval interests, national naval preferences are then promoted internationally in and out of the United Nations law of the sea negotiations.

If there is to be a new ocean order acceptable to most countries, there will have to be a reconciliation of competing maritime interests, including a reconciliation of naval interests. Since every nation prizes its sovereignty and security, compromises about issues concerning sea power are bound to be made carefully and probably with some hesitation. But without an accommodation of differing national naval interests, it is unlikely that any new law of the sea will emerge in practice.

Mere formal agreement by some or most states will not be enough. No effective law of the sea will be possible unless most ocean users respect whatever new rules are created. In the 19th century, the theory and practice of the law of the sea were so close that a real ocean order existed without formal conventions. If theory and practice are to coincide again, states will have to perceive that their best interests are served by a general obedience to international maritime norms. Thus a reconciliation of national ocean interests is vital not only for treaty drafting but for order itself. Order is a worthwhile goal both because it diminishes the loss of life and resources incumbent in strife and because it is the best way to ensure reasonable use of the oceans. One of the pillars on which the order must rest is an accommodation of different national sea power interests.

The law of the sea is the creature of international order, reflecting patterns of compromise and consensus, insofar as they exist, among the competing and complementary interests of states. Since security interests are vital to every country, it is only reasonable to expect that states will consider sea power when devising ocean policy. It would be remarkable if a workable legal order for the oceans did *not* accommodate national naval interests.

Sea power influences the development of the law of the sea not only by imposing the need to reconcile naval interests in international negotiations, but when naval force is used to advance national claims to international law of the sea. The law of the sea can be developed both by convention and by custom. Outside of the development of the law of the sea in the Third United Nations Law of the Sea Conference and in other diplomatic meetings, states attempt to develop customary law of the sea, making claims and counterclaims in their actual maritime practice. Navies often have a role in this process of customary law making.

All these aspects of the relationship between sea power and the law of the sea receive more detailed attention in the chapters that follow. The first four chapters deal with the naval interests and ocean policies of the four principal naval powers: the United States, the Soviet Union, Great Britain, and France. Each of these chapters considers the nation's naval interests in law of the sea issues, studies the role of the navy in national ocean policy making, and shows the extent to which national ocean policy reflects naval interests. Chapter 5 traces the naval interests and the legal positions of coastal navy states, countries which sometimes oppose the proposals of the naval powers. Chapter 6 is devoted to the ways in which navies and naval interests influence the development of the law of the sea. The seventh chapter charts some courses for the reconciliation of naval interests in a new international ocean order.

Sea Power and the Law of the Sea

1

The United States

United States Naval Interests in Law of the Sea Issues

From the beginning of the current law of the sea negotiations in 1967, the United States Navy has recognized that it has broad interests in a wide range of law of the sea issues.[1] Three specific legal issues, however, are of special importance for United States naval operations: passage through straits, transit along coasts, and military use of the deep seabed. The naval significance of these issues can be seen highlighted against the four missions of the United States Navy as officially established in 1970 by Admiral Elmo R. Zumwalt, Jr., then Chief of Naval Operations, and as elaborated in 1974 by Vice Admiral Stansfield Turner, then President of the Naval War College.[2] The four missions are strategic deterrence, sea control, projection of power ashore, and naval presence. Let us first briefly consider these missions and the forces available for their accomplishment.

Strategic deterrence is the most important United States naval mission. Its objectives are:

—To deter all-out attack on the United States or its allies;
—To face any potential aggressor contemplating less than all-out attack with unacceptable risk; and
—To maintain a stable political environment within which the threat of agression or coercion against the United States or its allies is minimized.[3]

Although all naval forces might be considered to be contributions to the maintenance of a stable political environment, the chief means the United States Navy uses to deter all-out or less than all-out attack on the United States and its allies is the Polaris/Poseidon system of nuclear submarines armed with intercontinental ballistic missiles, SSBNs. The United States has a fleet of 41 SSBNs: 5 "George Washington" class and 5 "Ethan Allen" class submarines armed with the Polaris A-3 missile with a range of 2500 nautical miles, and 31 "Lafayette" class submarines armed either with the Polaris A-3 or with the heavier and more accurate Poseidon C-3 missile with a range again of 2500 miles. Ten new SSBNs carrying the new Trident missile are authorized for construction, and the Trident system, which should be in commission by 1979 to 1980, will have a missile range of over 4500 miles. By the late 1970s over 5000 of the United States' 8000 strategic offensive warheads will be aboard the SSBN fleet, the remainder to be found on land-based missiles or aboard manned bombers.[4] The special advantage of the SSBN, accounting for its importance in the United States strategic deterrence plan, is that the submarine can stay submerged for 60 days. Because of the current state of the art of antisubmarine warfare, the SSBN while submerged is virtually invisible to enemy detection. Former Secretary of Defense Schlesinger considers the SSBN to be the most secure element of the United States nuclear deterrent.[5]

The rest of the United States naval fleet is mostly committed to the other three missions: sea control, projection of power ashore, and naval presence. Sea control is defined as ensuring industrial supplies, reinforcing and resupplying military forces engaged overseas, providing wartime economic and military supplies to allies, and providing safety for naval forces in the projection of power ashore role.[6] Sea control is the naval mission closest to the classical role for sea power as propounded by Admiral Mahan at the turn of the century. It means keeping sea lanes open for one's own side while denying them to the enemy. Especially crucial may be the control of choke points such as straits where maritime passage can be easily impeded. The projection of power ashore mission includes amphibious assault, naval bombardment, and tactical air.[7] All these permit naval forces to participate in wars on land and can be particularly useful when a nation does not station troops on foreign soil but still chooses to maintain the capability for foreign operations. Naval presence is termed "suasion" by one author in his study of the political uses of sea power.[8] Naval presence may be only "showing the flag," demonstrating a nation's concern and interest in another region. But naval presence may also include the threatened application of another of the naval missions, especially the threat of some sort of projection of power ashore. As such, it can be used in attempts to sway the policies of other countries.

For the three conventional missions, the 1974–1975 edition of *Jane's Fighting Ships* shows the United States naval force at about 700 ships.[9] These vessels include 15 aircraft carriers (more than all carriers of all other navies combined), about 200 major surface combatants (cruisers, destroyers, and frigates), about 70 fleet and patrol submarines, and more than 400 other craft (e.g., minesweepers, amphibious craft, supply ships, and patrol boats). In addition, unlike the other maritime powers, the United States maintains a separate Coast Guard, which is armed and which operates as part of the Navy in times of national emergency. The Coast Guard is bigger and more powerful than the navies of most other nations and operates some 40 surface combatant-type ships and about 200 other vessels. The United States Navy's forces are unrivalled for their ability for sea control and projection of power ashore. Despite the Soviet naval challenge, most observers rank the United States Navy as the most powerful afloat.[10]

The first legal issue which affects the effectiveness of the United States Navy is passage through straits, specifically international straits. International straits are those straits "between one part of the high seas and another part of the high seas or the territorial sea of a foreign state."[11] International straits 6 miles wide or less have been entirely overlapped by traditional territorial seas of 3 miles. Passage through these narrow international straits has been governed by the rules of innocent passage. Passage through straits wider than 6 miles, however, has not usually been regulated by coastal states because these wider straits include a zone of high seas where normal freedoms of the high seas pertain. Since many states now claim territorial seas of 12 miles, straits between 6 and 24 miles wide might pass into territorial waters and under the rules of innocent passage. There are some 121 such straits, including some of the most important waterways, such as the straits of Gibraltar, Dover, Hormuz, Bab el Mandeb, and Malacca.[12]

If these additional straits were governed by innocent passage rules, there might well be serious ramifications for United States naval operations, because of the power and authority given to coastal states to regulate passage through straits by these rules. Passage is considered innocent "so long as it is not prejudicial to the peace, good order, or security of the coastal state."[13] No state willingly concedes to another the determination of its security. The coastal state, therefore, has considerable discretion over the passage of foreign warships within its territorial waters. Colombos, the author of the classic English-language text on the law of the sea, puts it this way:

> The riparian state [bordering straits] is, however, entitled to take all precautions required for its security: for instance, in limiting the number of ships of war allowed to use the strait at the same time or the length of their stay there.[14]

Furthermore, the 1958 Geneva Conventions provide that in innocent passage "[s]ubmarines are required to navigate on the surface and show their flags."[15] There is no right of overflight permitted over territorial waters as there is over the high seas. Some states, such as the Soviet Union, require prior notification of warships that pass through straits within territorial waters.[16] Altogether, then, there are a large number of potential restrictions on naval operations through straits under innocent passage rules that would not exist if the old rules of high seas passage continued. The effect of these potential restrictions can be studied most easily on a mission-by-mission basis.

A comprehensive examination of the impact of innocent passage regimes for international straits between 6 and 24 miles wide on United States SSBN operations was presented in a 1974 article by Professor Osgood of Johns Hopkins University.[17] Of the 121 straits affected, he examined the 16 which might be of strategic importance for SSBN passage. Five of these are Caribbean straits (Old Bahamas Channel, Dominica, Martinique, Saint Lucia Channel, and Saint Vincent Passage) that he considers unimportant because other available straits are wider than 24 miles and because the Caribbean is not an essential launching area. Bab el Mandeb between the Red Sea and the Gulf of Aden, Hormuz between the Persian Gulf and the Indian Ocean, and Dover between the Atlantic and the North Sea are dismissed because sites can be targeted equally easily from elsewhere. Western Chosen is alongside the friendly states of Korea and Japan and is not essential because the neighboring strait between the Sea of Japan and the Yellow Sea, Tshushima, is 25 miles wide. The Bering Straits pose no problem because the United States is one of the coastal states. The Kennedy-Robeson Channels to the Arctic are under the control of our ally, Canada. Neither Malacca nor Sunda between the South China Sea and the Indian Ocean are safe routes for submarine passage. This leaves only two more Indonesian straits, Ombai-Wetar and Lombok, and the straits of Gibraltar. These three are under the control of friendly governments and, even so, would not be important once the Trident system with its longer ranges is deployed.

Osgood's analysis is persuasive and tends to prove the proposition that inclusion of 6- to 24-mile-wide straits within innocent passage regimes would not greatly weaken the United States Navy's SSBN nuclear deterrent. Still, some arguments remain which would persuade the Navy to oppose innocent passage rules on grounds of strategic deterrence. First, one cannot always assume the goodwill of now friendly governments. Even allies may exact greater political and economic concessions in exchange for unimpeded submarine passage. Furthermore, even after the introduction of the Trident system, shorter-range SSBNs will still be in use and their mobility will remain at stake. Free passage of straits will give the older and even the newer SSBNs all that much more room to maneuver and evade detection. The Navy, therefore, can be expected to resist any effort to impose innocent passage regimes which might require that the submarines on strategic deterrence missions surface or give prior notice. Either requirement would make it easier for an antagonist to locate and, thereby, threaten the submarines.

More serious problems still are posed by innocent passage regimes for straits with regard to the Navy's three conventional missions. The key straits are Gilbraltar and the Indonesian passages. Gilbraltar is absolutely vital for United States naval operations in the Mediterranean. The United States Sixth Fleet has been active in fulfilling all three conventional roles since its formation and deployment in 1948.[18] At first perceived as a naval presence to help symbolize the United States commitment to resist Soviet influence in southern Europe, the Sixth Fleet's major role has remained one of presence, demonstrating United States support for the North Atlantic Treaty Organization and for other friendly states around the Mediterranean. But the Sixth Fleet has also projected power ashore, for example, during the 1958 Lebanon Crisis, and has been instrumental in the control of sea lanes, such as during the resupply of Israel during the 1973 Arab-Israeli War. For the Sixth Fleet the only alternative to Gibraltar is the Suez Canal, which not only is under the control of a country not always linked with United States interests but which opens on the Indian Ocean far from the home ports of United States warships.

The other vital passages—the Indonesian straits of Malacca, Sunda, Lombok, and Ombai-Wetar—cut over a week of transit time for United States vessels of the Seventh Fleet traveling between the Pacific and the Indian Oceans. Although United States naval operations in the Indian Ocean are not of the same magnitude as those in the Mediterranean, they are beginning to awaken controversy in the United States. Without attempting to predict the outcome of the debate about the United States naval presence in the Indian Ocean, it is safe to say that the United States naval forces there will, to some degree, continue to be important for supporting allies and friends (especially those with oil), for countering the Soviet naval presence, and for protecting sea lanes and communications.[19]

Another strait, Hormuz, which leads to the Persian Gulf should be mentioned. It is of some, but not vital, importance to the United States Navy. Three United States vessels have been deployed in the Gulf since 1949.[20] Although the force is symbolic of the United States presence in the Middle East, it is far less significant than the presence of either the Sixth or Seventh Fleets.

Not surprisingly, coastal straits states such as Spain and Indonesia have been among the leaders in the attempt to extend territorial seas over international straits. The more the coastal state can control neighboring straits, the greater its bargaining strength in bilateral or multilateral negotiations. Although the United States Navy would probably have the physical capacity to transit straits in times of crisis, the narrow waters of a strait are excellent for the exertion of power by a weaker naval state, which can use land-based air power and weapons and coastal patrol boats to good advantage against larger naval units. Furthermore, in a crisis situation, the United States (or any country, for that matter) strives to minimize the hostility of third-party states, including coastal states that might well sympathize with states along straits which complain of naval passage.

A threat of impeded passage could reduce the effectiveness of the United States naval presence in the Mediterranean and the

Indian Ocean. Vigorous protests or physical resistance could delay resupplying forces, postpone an amphibious assault, or divert ships intended for projection of power ashore. The diversion of ships could prove to be significant since the need to protect access through straits would reduce the force available for the accomplishment of the primary mission.

But apart from ensuring access to the Mediterranean and the Indian Ocean, passage through straits is not vital for the United States Navy. Facing the Atlantic and the Pacific, the United States has clear sailing to most of the world's ocean space. Comparatively, it has much easier access than its principal opponent, the Soviet Navy, which would, as seen below, be hindered much more greatly by restrictive straits regimes. The United States, however, has defined its law of the sea interests absolutely and not comparatively, a point considered again in Chapter 7. United States naval interest in the legal regimes of international straits is rooted, therefore, in the naval interest to operate freely in the Mediterranean and the Indian Ocean, principally, but not entirely, to fulfill conventional naval missions.

The second legal issue, transit along coasts, arises because of the claims, already mentioned, by coastal states to extend their territorial seas and other zones of national control. Given traditional 3-mile territorial seas, navies could operate freely very near to the land of other countries. This transit right gave navies the opportunity to show the flag near foreign states and to use the vast areas of the high seas for wartime activities just off the coasts of neutral states. Within territorial waters naval vessels are subject to the rules of aforementioned innocent passage, whereby the coastal state has the right to require a warship to leave if the warship fails to comply with the regulations of the coastal state.[21]

Although most states now seek no more than 12-mile territorial seas, which would be no great restriction on most naval operations other than passage through international straits narrower than 24 miles, there is fear that these jurisdictions might "creep." It seems likely that 200-mile economic zones will be established and that these zones will give coastal states exclusive economic rights. But if jurisdiction creeps, it might come to emcompass some form or other of control over the transit of naval vessels. Some 30 percent of the oceans come within national jurisdiction with 200-mile zones.[22] 200-mile zones would entirely cover the Mediterranean, the North Sea, the Persian Gulf, and the South China Sea.[23] Thus, the Navy is concerned not only with broad territorial seas but also with creeping 200-mile economic zones.

The greater the extent of territorial seas or seas which have somehow crept to include regulation of naval operations, the lesser the domain in which navies may transit freely. Such regulations could significantly restrict the United States naval presence role. The flag, after all, is considerably more difficult to see at 200 than at 3 or 12 miles. The operations of the Sixth Fleet might be entirely at the discretion of regional states, which could divide the Mediterranean among themselves. Some states might encourage while others oppose United States naval activities, leaving a patchwork of possible seas for United States naval operations. The same could be true in the South China Sea and the Persian Gulf. Coastal states could begin, too, to regulate naval intelligence-gathering activities within the 200-mile zone, and naval research is an important part of the support for all naval missions.

Sea control and projection of power ashore would also be affected. Although the Navy would operate within the waters of friendly and enemy states in times of conflict; it might be inhibited from operating within extended zones of neutral states seeking to remain uninvolved. Thus, it could well become more difficult for the Navy to resupply an ally or launch an attack. There would be a patchwork effect in wartime similar to that in peacetime.

But there is a positive side to extended state zones and restrictions on naval transit along coasts. The role of strategic deterrence might well be enhanced. The United States and its allies (e.g., Canada, Great Britain, Japan, and Australia) would gain large expanses of oceans from which they might prohibit the warships of the Soviet Union. This could reduce the threat of Soviet antisubmarine activities and thus add to the invulnerability of the United States SSBN nuclear deterrent.

The third law of the sea issue which affects United States naval missions is military use of the deep seabed. On December 17, 1970, the General Assembly of the United Nations adopted Resolution 2749 (XXV) by a vote of 108 in favor (including the United States) to none against, with 14 abstentions.[24] This resolution declared that the deep seabed was the common heritage of mankind and that it should be governed by some sort of international regime. Although the law of the sea negotiations have not yet yielded an international regime for the seabed, the *Informal Single Negotiating Text* which issued from the 1975 Geneva session of the Law of the Sea Conference includes a provision that the deep seabed "shall be reserved exclusively for peaceful purposes."[25]

From the point of view of the United States Navy, it is important that the peaceful use of the seabed not be taken to mean the prohibition of seabed listening devices.[26] These devices are a means the Navy uses to detect the passage of submarines and are thus an important part of the United States naval effort to protect United States SSBNs, surface ships, and maritime commerce from enemy submarine attack. In the negotiations leading to the drafting of the 1971 Seabed Arms Control Treaty, the United States was successful in eliminating wording similar to that of the *Informal Single Negotiating Text* and substituting instead a prohibition on weapons of mass destruction. Under these terms, seabed listening devices are permitted since, although military, they are not themselves weapons, much less weapons of mass destruction.

From the standpoint of its own mission structure, then, the United States Navy is well served by the traditional order of the freedoms of the high seas. Passage rights through straits facilitate some SSBN operations and are crucial for conventional operations in theaters such as the Mediterranean and Indian Ocean. Free transit rights along coasts up to a narrow band of coastal state control give the Navy room to conduct sea control and projection of power ashore roles and good scope for an active naval presence role. Freedom to implant seabed listening devices aids in antisubmarine operations.

But it is important to evaluate the possible benefits of different regimes, too. One such advantage is the greater protection extended coastal state zones might afford to SSBN activities. Other advantages come from the relatively worse disadvantages faced by the Soviet Navy by restrictions on freedoms of the high seas and from the improved situations secured thereby by allied navies. These comparative analyses are better considered later, after examining the naval interests of other countries. At this point, it suffices to note that the United States Navy perceives that freedoms of the high seas aid in the accomplishment of the Navy's four missions. It can, accordingly, be expected that the Navy will promote high seas freedoms in the United States policy process.

The Role of Naval Interests in the United States Ocean Policy Process

Naval interests are only some of many interests that must be coordinated in the drafting of United States ocean policy. Probably no country has quite so many different ocean interests and so many institutions to promote them. There are some 40 federal executive bureaus and agencies, some 33 congressional subcommittees, 30 states, and a wide range of commercial interests including fishing, oil and gas, and the merchant marine, all concerned with the development of United States maritime policy.[27]

Although these diverse interests deal with an equally broad range of maritime policy decisions, naval interests (straits, coastal transit, and the deep seabed) are chiefly related to policy made by the federal government either concerning the ongoing international law of the sea negotiations or concerning any extension of United States national ocean jurisdiction. The actors concerned with these decisions can be conveniently grouped into three levels: the executive branch, Congress, and nongovernmental institutions (including private corporations and interest groups, the press, and the universities).

Each of these three levels has an impact on United States national ocean policy, but since the responsibility for conducting international negotiations rests with the President, it is not surprising that the executive branch is the crucial level for decision making concerning the law of the sea negotiations. Although the Senate will have to ratify any eventual law of the sea treaty, Congress has been more concerned with the second area of decision making, the extension of United States coastal control. Nongovernmental bodies and individuals have been influential to the degree to which they have been able to persuade executive or congressional elements to promote their viewpoints.

The major role that the United States naval interests have played in the ocean policy process has been within the executive branch. The picture of the executive-level ocean policy process has been best painted in a series of articles written by Professor Hollick of Johns Hopkins University, who has concluded that "[s]ince 1970, law of the sea policy in the United States has been the product of intensive negotiations among evenly matched opposing domestic and bureaucratic interests."[28] The focus for these negotiations has been the Inter-Agency Task Force on the Law of the Sea, which was created in 1970 to coordinate the interests of the executive bureaus and agencies most concerned with law of the sea questions. Fourteen institutions are represented: the departments of State, Defense, Interior, Commerce, Treasury, Justice, and Transportation; the National Security Council; the National Science Foundation; the Central Intelligence Agency; the Office of Management and Budget; the United States Mission to the United Nations; the Environmental Protection Agency; and the Council on Environmental Quality.[29] The Task Force has always been chaired by the Department of State, first by John R. Stevenson, then Legal Adviser, and beginning in 1973 by John Norton Moore, the head of a newly created Law of the Sea Office at the State Department.[30] The Task Force is an instrument to facilitate consensus building among the various executive-branch bureaucracies more than it is a centralized decision-making body. Functionally it inherits the informal means of consensus building used before the Task Force's creation.

The Inter-Agency Task Force includes both a civilian and military representative of naval interests. In 1975, Stuart P. French, the Director of the Pentagon's Law of the Sea Task Force, and Rear Admiral Max K. Morris, the Joint Chiefs of Staff Representative for Law of the Sea Matters, were Task Force participants. Individuals from the International Law Division of the Navy's Judge Advocate General's Office and from the Ocean Affairs Division of the Deputy Chief of Naval Operations (Plans and Policy) have been brought in to support the Department of Defense and Joint Chiefs of Staff representatives. Within the Pentagon, the Defense Advisory Committee on the Law of the Sea has coordinated the input from all branches of the service.

Although the consensus-building techniques of executive-branch ocean policy decision making have always left the door open, more or less, for various inputs, Hollick asserts that national security interests had priority before 1971.[31] This was due both to a reasonably small number of actively concerned bureaus and agencies and to State Department support for naval positions. After 1971, however, increased participation from other sectors led to a greater proportionality between other inputs and those of the Defense Department.[32]

Within the executive branch, naval interests have clashed with other interests that favored extended coastal state jurisdictions. The Navy has generally opposed efforts to unilaterally expand United States ocean jurisdiction lest other nations follow the example of the United States and thus endanger naval mobility. Between 1967 and 1972, the Defense Department found itself in opposition to the Interior Department which, with the United States oil industry, supported broader claims to the continental shelf.[33] As discussed more fully in the next section, naval interests won the early battle on the continental shelf when President Nixon, in 1970, endorsed limits of 200 meters in depth for continental shelf claims, but finally lost the war when the United States followed the suit of other countries and expressed willingness to accept national jurisdiction over the shelf beyond 200 meters.

A second executive-level dispute began in 1973 concerning the exploitation of minerals on the deep seabed. The Treasury Department supports the position of United States hard-rock exploiters and seeks United States guarantees for deep-sea mining of manganese nodules. The Defense Department, on the other hand, is more willing to accept an international regime for deep-sea exploitation in negotiated exchange for navigation rights.[34]

The Congressional Research Service has pointed out how difficult it has been to reconcile the diverse United States maritime interests.[35] Certainly, the interagency battles in the United States concerning law of the sea policy have been noteworthy for their persistence and divisiveness. But the battles are also remarkable for their publicity. No other country displays such well-reported disputes. This may be due not only to the relatively free disclosure of governmental processes in the United States, but also to the fact that the United States, more than almost any other nation, has very important coastal and distant-water interests.

Battles about United States ocean policy are compounded by disputes between the executive branch and Congress. The history of congressional criticism of United States ocean policy extends unbroken at least into the Eisenhower administration.[36] Congress has often complained that the executive branch has failed to manage ocean affairs properly, and there is a long tradition of congressional investigations into the formulation of United States ocean policy. Congress has tended to be influenced more than the executive by domestic economic interests and less by naval interests. Congress has also favored the unilateral extension of United States jurisdiction into the oceans, first by proposing to extend United States fishing limits and second by showing a greater willingness to authorize protection for unilateral United States mining activities.[37]

Given the unilateralist leanings of Congress, the Defense Department has sought to hold the executive ocean policy fort when it has been brought under congressional fire. Testimony before congressional committees, some of which is presented in the next section, has attempted to dissuade Congress from moving to extend United States jurisdiction, arguing that the move would snowball and other states would come to restrict United States naval mobility. Economic interests, however, have had better luck with Congress.

Outside the executive and Congress, the Defense Department has not attempted to promote naval interests very broadly. Although some articles have appeared supporting naval positions in the law of the sea debate, these have been largely in journals for the Navy professional, whom one supposes to be already inclined toward the naval perspective.[38] It is likely that the decision not to make an appeal for naval interests outside of the federal government is motivated in part, at least, by the desire to be a cooperative member of the executive-level decision-making team and by the decision that the effectiveness of any public appeal would be limited by the unpopularity of military causes after Vietnam. Another factor may be that the promotion of naval interests in nongovernmental forums has been relatively unnecessary since United States ocean policy has, at least until recently, been generally favorable for naval concerns.

The Reflection of Naval Interests in United States Ocean Policy

The importance given to naval interests in drafting United States ocean policy is not a new development. In 1958 at the First United Nations Conference on the Law of the Sea, Arthur H. Dean, the Chairman of the United States delegation, put the protection of the 3-mile limit as the "first goal" of the United States.[39] Such a position accommodated United States commercial shipping, but shipping interests, strangely, were not and still are not at all influential in United States ocean policy making. Naval mobility rationales were most usually offered to justify the United States stand for freedoms of the high seas.[40]

Promotion of naval interests was clearly also an aim of the 1970 United States ocean policy, as announced by President Nixon in a major speech on the oceans. This policy granted the willingness of the United States to accept a 12-mile territorial sea, provided that free transit through straits and protection of other freedoms of the high seas were ensured.[41] This 1970 policy remains the underlying basis of the official United States position in the law of the sea negotiations. The policy's philosophical foundation is a distinction drawn between resource and nonresource uses of the oceans. This philosophical foundation was perhaps best stated in an important elaboration of the 1970 policy position by John R. Stevenson, then United States representative to the Seabed Committee, in 1972:

Ocean uses can be divided into two broad categories: resource uses and non-resource uses. The first group principally concerns fishing and seabed resources. The non-resource uses include such important interests as navigation and overflight, scientific research and the preservation of the ocean environment.[42]

Naval uses are non-resource uses. Stevenson's speech made it clear that the United States would not sacrifice limited territorial seas and free transit through straits:

The view of my delegation on non-resource uses has been clearly stated on a number of occasions. It is our candid opinion that there is no possibility for agreement on a breadth of the territorial sea other than 12 nautical miles. The United States and others have also made it clear that their vital interests require that agreement on a 12-mile territorial sea be coupled with an agreement on free transit of straits used for international navigation and these remain basic elements of our national policy which we will not sacrifice.[43]

The remainder and bulk of Stevenson's speech is devoted to a presentation of the United States position on resources and is aimed to "dispel" the "impression" that the United States and others "can be expected to sacrifice in these negotiations basic elements of their national policy on resources."[44] But in this "impression" there has been an important element of truth. The United States has been willing to compromise resource policy in exchange for concessions on non-resource uses. One need only return to the 1970 Nixon policy to see this trade-off. Despite the demands of the oil companies and the Department of the Interior for an extension of the jurisdiction of the United States to the limits of the continental shelf,[45] the 1970 policy statement proposed renunciation of "all national claims over the natural resources of the seabed beyond the point where the high seas reach a depth of 200 metres (218.8 yards), and would agree to regard these resources as the common heritage of mankind."[46] Instead of providing for United States licensing of seabed mining as the mineral companies sought,[47] the 1970 statement provided for an international regime which would administer the ocean floor beyond the continental margin and also for a trusteeship zone to be administered by the coastal state. In the trusteeship zone, between 200 meters and the deep seabed, the coastal state would contribute "substantial" mineral royalties to "an appropriate international development agency for assistance of developing countries."[48]

Stevenson was right in saying that the United States has never been willing to sacrifice resource uses. Nixon's 1970 speech, for example, insists on "due protection for the integrity of investments."[49] But the United States has been willing to give more in terms of resource uses than in terms of non-resource uses. In a 1972 speech to the American Bar Association, Ambassador Stevenson referred to five basic components of United States ocean policy: territorial sea and straits, fisheries, seabed resources, scientific research, and environmental protection.[50] Only in the first area, that most important to the Navy, did he say that the United States was "insisting" on its position. The words used to describe the United States stand in the other four areas were "proposed," "supports," and "vigorously seeking." The single case of insistence was explained in terms of military and commercial importance and that the right of innocent passage through straits was "no longer a satisfactory guarantee."[51]

Although, when discussing the need for free transit, the representatives of the United States often link naval and merchant marine concerns, it is the naval interest which is foremost. The merchant marine has never been a significant participant in the United States interagency negotiations.[52] Naval interests, on the other hand, are considerable enough to countervail the very influential economic interests of oil and hard-rock mineral exploiters.

The importance of naval interests for United States ocean policy is shown by the often reemphasized United States stand on free transit through straits. As Moore, the Chairman of the Inter-

Agency Task Force on the Law of the Sea, put it at the Caracas session of the Law of the Sea Conference in 1974,

The United States delegation has stated on numerous occasions the central importance that we attach to a satisfactory treaty regime of unimpeded transit through and over straits used for international navigation. Indeed, for states bordering as well as states whose ships and aircraft transit such straits, there could not be a successful Law of the Sea Conference unless this question is satisfactorily resolved.[53]

Naval interests have also figured in the defense of executive-branch policy before Congress. Executive-level representatives have consistently argued against unilateral extensions of United States ocean jurisdiction, stating that such unilateral action could trigger more claims by other states and thereby threaten United States naval access. An example of such testimony is that of General George S. Brown, Chairman of the Joint Chiefs of Staff, concerning the proposed 200-mile fishing limit in 1974:

In my judgement, enactment of the proposed legislation would seriously erode the prospect for a broadly based multilateral treaty putting to rest the wide range of increasingly contentious ocean issues. Enactment of the proposed legislation would be a dramatic and highly visible reversal of past U.S. policy. For the United States to adopt unilateralism at this juncture would seriously undercut the credibility of U.S. negotiators not only on the fisheries issue, but also on our basic commitment to international agreement. This unilateral action could result in an erosion of the world's perception of our other essential objectives such as unimpeded transit through and over straits, which we have identified as both cornerstones of our policy and essential elements of an acceptable solution.[54]

With regard to the second issue of naval importance, transit along coasts, the United States has again taken an international position close to that of naval interests. The United States has indicated its willingness to accept a 12-mile territorial sea and a 200-mile economic zone, but has conditioned its acceptance of these extensions on the preservation of transit rights and other non-resource uses beyond 12 miles. As Stevenson explained in his opening speech at Caracas in 1974,

Our willingness and that of many other delegations to accept a 200-mile outer limit for the economic zone depends on the concurrent negotiation and acceptance of correlative coastal state duties. The coastal rights we contemplate comprise full regulatory jurisdiction over exploration and exploitation of seabed resources, non-resource drilling, fishing for coastal and anadromous species, and installations constructed for economic purposes. The rights of other states include freedom of navigation, overflight, and other non-resource uses.[55]

Thus the United States has taken a firm stand against the economic zone creeping into a 200-mile territorial sea. Later in the Caracas negotiations, Stevenson emphasized that United States acceptance of a 200-mile economic zone was strictly contingent upon the recognition of the preservation of high seas freedoms for non-resource uses.[56]

In law of the sea negotiations relating to the third issue of concern to the Navy, military use of the deep seabed, the official ocean policy of the United States has remained steadfastly opposed to the prohibition of all military use of the ocean floor. Once again, the United States position distinguishes between resource and non-resource uses. The United States proposed to Committee I of the Caracas session that "the mandate of the authority [for the deep seabed] should be to control only activities in the area which were directly related to the exploration and exploitation of seabed resources."[57]

The discussion above has demonstrated that naval interests have been reflected in United States ocean policy. The United States position on straits, transit along coasts, and military use of the deep seabed facilitates perceived naval interests. But naval interests have been less successful in preserving negotiating chips to trade with other countries in the law of the sea bargaining sessions.

If, at first, it seemed that assurances of naval access might be secured in exchange for United States acceptance of 12-mile territorial seas, such an exchange is out of date today. So many countries claim 12-mile zones that 12 miles is probably already the territorial sea established by custom. It would be fruitless for the United States to withhold its consent to them.

And, if later it seemed that naval access might be had in exchange for agreement to a 200-mile economic zone, this exchange, too, is nearly out of date. Executive branch spokesmen have long opposed congressional action to extend United States fishing limits to 200 miles:

[U]nilateral action in this area by the United States could trigger damaging unilateral claims by other nations, thereby affecting U.S. national interests in navigation and overflight, protection of the marine environment, and marine scientific research.[58]

But the House of Representatives passed a 200-mile fishing limit in October 1975, by a vote of 208 to 101.[59] And the Senate did the same in January 1976, by a vote of 77 to 19.[60] Even the Senate Armed Services Committee voted 9 to 7 to approve a 200-mile limit, despite testimony for the Joint Chiefs of Staff which stressed that it would inspire similar unilateral claims by other states and threaten the United States naval presence in the Mediterranean.[61] Under election year pressure, President Ford agreed to sign a bill for 200-mile fishing limits if the date for its institution were set back to March 1, 1977, hopefully after the completion of successful negotiations at the Law of the Sea Conference.[62] It is now impossible for United States delegates to argue that the United States will accept 200-mile economic zones only if there are guarantees for passage through straits and transit along coasts. The United States is committed to a 200-mile zone for itself regardless of the results of the Conference, and it would be inconceivable for the United States to claim its own 200-mile zone and deny the same to other states.

Of course, the United States need not and has not retreated from its insistence that the 200-mile zone be only for economic control and not impede the transit of warships and merchant vessels. Nor need the country abandon its stand that there be free transit through international straits. It is only that there are fewer concessions which the United States might now make in exchange for these rights. United States economic interests have now put themselves on a par with United States naval interests, winning the fight in Congress after the Navy won the battle in the executive branch.

Notes

1. Wilfred A. Hearn, "The Fourth Dimension of Seapower: Ocean Technology and International Law: Introduction," *JAG Journal* 22 (September–October–November 1967):25.

2. Stansfield Turner, "Missions of the U.S. Navy," *Naval War College Review* 26 (March–April 1974):2–17.

3. Ibid., p. 5.

4. John E. Moore (ed.), *Jane's Fighting Ships 1974–1975* (London: Macdonald & Co., 1974), pp. 385–389 and 633.

5. U.S., Department of Defense, *Annual Defense Department Report: FY 1976 and FY 197T,* 1975, p. II-30.

6. Turner, "Missions of the U.S. Navy," p. 8.

7. Ibid., p. 10.

8. Edward N. Luttwak, *The Political Uses of Sea Power* (Baltimore: Johns Hopkins University Press, 1974), pp. 1–38.

9. Moore (ed.), *Jane's,* pp. 370 and 515. Current United States Navy estimates give United States naval strength at about 500 vessels, but since this analysis relies on *Jane's* for comparison with other fleets, *Jane's* figures will be used for the United States fleet as well.

10. "Full Ahead on Naval Spending," *Manchester Guardian Weekly* (London), 10 May 1975, p. 6; "CNO Tells Congress USN Still Number One—But Barely," *Naval Institute Proceedings* 102 (April 1976):114; "Data Show Navy Lead in Big Ships," *New York Times,* 3 May 1976, p. 5.

11. U.S., Department of State, "Convention on the Territorial Sea and the Contiguous Zone," T.I.A.S. No. 5639, Art. 16, Sec. 4.

12. U.S., Department of State, Office of the Geographer, *World Straits Affected by a 12-Mile Territorial Sea* (chart, 1971).

13. "Convention on the Territorial Sea and the Contiguous Zone," Art. 14, Sec. 4.

14. C. John Colombos, *The International Law of the Sea,* 4th rev. ed. (London: Longmans, 1961), p. 170.

15. "Convention on the Territorial Sea and the Contiguous Zone," Art. 14, Sec. 6.

16. U.S.S.R., Ministry of Defense, *Manual of International Maritime Law* (Moscow: Military Publishing House, 1966), Naval Intelligence Command Translation No. 2500 (a/b), p. 23.

17. Robert E. Osgood, "U.S. Security Interests in Ocean Law," *Ocean Development and International Law* 2 (Spring 1974):11–18.

18. P. A. Dur, "The U.S. Sixth Fleet: Search for Consensus," *Naval Institute Proceedings* 100 (April 1974):18–23.

19. D. C. F. Daniel, "Naval Presence and National Interests: The Case of the United States Navy in the Indian Ocean," paper presented to the Western Political Science Association, March 20, 1975, Seattle.

20. P. W. DeForth, "U.S. Naval Presence in the Persian Gulf," *Naval War College Review* 28 (Summer 1975):28–38.

21. "Convention on the Territorial Sea and the Contiguous Zone." Art. 23.

22. Arvid Pardo, "A Statement on the Future of the Law of the Sea in Light of Current Trends in Negotiations," *Ocean Development and International Law* 1 (Winter 1974):332.

23. U.S., Department of State, Office of the Geographer, *Global Effect of 200-Mile Nautical Mile Territorial Sea Claim* (chart, 1971).

24. United Nations, *UN Monthly Chronicle* 8 (January 1971):37–38.

25. United Nations, General Assembly, *Informal Single Negotiating Text* (A/CONF.62/WP.8/Part I), 1975, p. 4.

26. James A. Barry, Jr., "The Seabed Arms Control Issue, 1967–1971: A Superpower Symbiosis?" *Naval War College Review* 25 (September–October, 1972):87–101; Evan Luard, *The Control of the Sea-Bed* (London: Heinemann, 1974), pp. 97– 112.

27. Edward Wenk, Jr., *The Politics of the Ocean* (Seattle: University of Washington Press, 1972), p. 31.

28. Ann L. Hollick, "United States and Canadian Policy Processes in Law of the Sea," *San Diego Law Review* 12(3):536.

29. Ibid., pp. 536–537.

30. Ibid., p. 536.

31. Ann L. Hollick, "Seabeds Make Strange Politics," *Foreign Policy* (Winter 1972–1973):148–162.

32. Ibid., p. 164.

33. Ann L. Hollick, "Bureaucrats at Sea," in A. Hollick and R. Osgood (eds.), *New Era of Ocean Politics,* (Baltimore: Johns Hopkins University Press, 1974), pp. 1–3 and 15–40.

34. Ibid., pp. 1–4 and 52–64.

35. U.S., Library of Congress, Congressional Research Service, *Soviet Ocean Activities: A Preliminary Survey,* 1975, p. 81.

36. Wenk, *The Politics of the Ocean.*

37. "Senate Panel Wants Foreign Fishermen Kept 200 Miles Out," *Washington Post,* 23 September 1974, p. A5.

38. Hearn, "Ocean Technology and International Law;" "Law of the Sea Issue," *JAG Journal* 25 (December–January 1970–1971); E. L. Gallup, "Sovereignty of the Seas and the Effect upon Naval Strategy," *Marine Affairs Journal* No. 1 (1973):1–8; E. F. Oliver, "Malacca: Dire Straits," *Naval Institute Proceedings* 99 (April 1973):26–33; M. W. Janis, "Freedoms of the High Seas: An Impossibility?" *Naval Institute Proceedings* 100 (March 1974):112–114.

39. Arthur H. Dean, "The Geneva Conference on the Law of the Sea: What Was Accomplished," *American Journal of International Law* 52 (October 1958):610.

40. Ibid., pp. 610–611.

41. United Nations, General Assembly, *Announcement by President Nixon on United States Ocean Policy, Saturday, May 23, 1970* (A/AC.138/22), 1970.

42. U.S., U.S.I.A., Press Release, August 10, 1972, p. 1.

43. Ibid., p. 2.

44. Ibid., pp. 2–5.

45. Hollick, "Bureaucrats at Sea," pp. 15–40.

46. UN, *Announcement by President Nixon,* p. 2.

47. Hollick, "Bureaucrats at Sea," pp. 24–26.

48. UN, *Announcement by President Nixon,* pp. 2–3.

49. Ibid., p. 2.

50. John R. Stevenson, "Who Is to Control the Oceans: U.S. Policy and the Law of the Sea Conference," *International Lawyer* 6 (July 1972):465–477.

51. Ibid., p. 469.

52. Hollick, "Bureaucrats at Sea," p. 15.

53. U.S., Department of State, Press Release, July 22, 1974, p. 1.

54. U.S., Department of State, Press Release, October 8, 1974, p. 9.

55. U.S., Department of State, Press Release, July 11, 1974, p. 3.

56. United Nations, General Assembly, *Third United Nations Conference on the Law of the Sea Records* (A/CONF.62/C.2/SR.24), 1974, pp. 12–14.

57. Ibid. (A/CONF.62/C.1/SR.8), 1974, p. 22.

58. U.S., Department of State, Press Release, Statement by Kenneth Rush, Acting Secretary of State, May 3, 1974, p. 10.

59. "U.S. Fishing Zone of Within 200 Miles Is Voted by House," *Wall Street Journal,* 10 October 1975, p. 16.

60. "Senate Approves a 200-Mile Limit on Fishing Rights," *New York Times,* 29 January 1976, p. 1.

61. "Senate Panel Backs Bill on 200-Mile Fishing Zone," *Washington Post,* 4 December 1975, p. A2.

62. "Compromise Is Reached on 200-Mile U.S. Fishing Limit," *Washington Post,* 18 March 1976, p. A4: "Ford Signs Measure Setting Sea Limit," *New York Times,* 15 April 1976, p. 26.

2

The Soviet Union

Soviet Naval Interests in Law of the Sea Issues

That the modern Soviet Navy is concerned with law of the sea issues is clear from the importance given the law of the sea debate by the Commander-in-Chief of the Soviet Navy, Admiral S. G. Gorshkov, in a series of articles in 1972 to 1973 entitled "Navies in War and in Peace."[1] The first half of the final instalment is reserved for a consideration of law of the sea questions, in which it is indicated that the Soviet Navy is interested in the same three legal issues as the United States Navy: passage through straits, transit along coasts, and military use of the deep seabed. The naval relevance of these issues for the Soviet Union can be understood in terms of the missions and composition of the Soviet Navy. Turning to earlier numbers of "Navies in War and in Peace," we find that Gorshkov sets out three missions for his forces: defense of the homeland, sea denial, and naval presence.

The most important mission for Soviet sea power is defense of the homeland,[2] to which the Soviet Navy contributes in two fashions: with strategic deterrent and conventional defensive forces.[3] For strategic deterrence, the Soviet Navy has about 48 nuclear and 22 diesel submarines armed with nuclear intercontinental ballistic missiles: 22 diesel-powered "Golf" class submarines armed with the SS-N-4 missile with a short 300-nautical-mile range and the SS-N-5 missile with a 700-nautical-mile range; 9 nuclear powered "Hotel" class submarines with the SS-N-5; 33 nuclear-powered "Yankee" class submarines with the SS-N-6 with a 1300-nautical-mile range; and 6 nuclear-powered "Delta" class submarines with the much longer-ranged SS-N-8 missile with a 4200-nautical-mile range.[4] These forces are intended to deter nuclear attack from the United States and conventional attack on Russia's Asian and European frontiers.

For conventional defense, the Soviet Navy boasts roughly half of all the world's fleet and patrol submarines: 39 nuclear-powered and 28 diesel-powered cruise missile submarines, 30 nuclear-powered and 28 diesel-powered fleet submarines, and 230 diesel-powered patrol submarines, an awesome total of some 355 submarines in all.[5] These, along with the Soviet naval air arm, can be used as anticarrier forces to threaten the United States Navy's carrier-borne nuclear strike forces in the Mediterranean and in the Norwegian Sea. They may also be a threat of some degree to United States SSBN operations.[6]

These submarine forces are also useful in accomplishing the second role for Soviet sea power, sea denial. Gorshkov visualizes Soviet sea denial largely in terms of denying the United States Navy, that he calls "an instrument of imperialist policy," access to foreign theaters, e.g., the Mediterranean, the Middle East, the Far East, and South Asia.[7] But there is no doubt that these forces also have the capability of interdicting the West's maritime commerce and lines of communication.[8]

The third naval role for the Soviet Union, naval presence, is justified by Gorshkov as follows:

Owing to the high mobility and endurance of its combatants, the Navy possesses the capability to vividly demonstrate the economic and military might of a country beyond its borders during peacetime.[9]

Gorshkov also sees naval presence as an important prestige symbol, a sign that the country with significant naval power holds "a definite place among the other powers."[10] To fulfill the naval presence role and to contribute to defense of the homeland and sea denial, the Soviet Navy sails the world's largest surface fleet: about 200 surface combatants and more than 1000 other craft, including two aircraft carriers now under construction.[11]

Compared with the missions and composition of the United States Navy, the Soviet Navy shares the roles of strategic deterrence and naval presence and is well equipped to carry them out. However, without a strong carrier force and with a weaker amphibious capability, the Soviet Navy is less able to execute sea control or projection of power ashore roles. Instead, the Soviet Navy is structured for sea denial so as to deprive the United States Navy of its sea control and projection of power ashore capabilities. But considering both its missions and its makeup, the Soviet Navy is in the superpower class of the United States Navy.

To the great disadvantage of the Soviet Navy, however, the Soviet Union has considerably less easy access to the oceans than does the United States. Of the Soviet Navy's four fleets, only the Northern Fleet, based in Murmansk, has an ice-free, straits-free route to the high seas. The Baltic Fleet not only is ice-plagued in winter but also must pass through the Danish straits to reach the North Sea and then through Dover or through the Britain/Norway gap to reach the Atlantic. The Black Sea Fleet must pass through the Turkish straits to reach the Mediterranean and then the straits of Gibraltar to reach the Atlantic or Suez to reach the Indian Ocean. Most of the Pacific Fleet must pass through the straits of the Sea of Japan to reach the Pacific. These geographical conditions have a real impact on Soviet naval interests in law of the sea issues.

The Soviet Navy's position on the first legal issue, passage through straits, is stated forthrightly by Gorshkov, who advocates free transit and overflight for all ships and aircraft through and over international straits.[12] The rationale for this Soviet naval attitude toward straits is principally the protection of the conventional defensive, sea denial, and naval presence roles. As with the United States Navy, the Soviet Navy's strategic deterrent role would not be much affected by innocent passage regimes for straits between 6 and 24 miles wide. A Naval Postgraduate School study by Lieutenant Commander J. P. Deaton explained that the offensive strategic submarines of the Soviet Navy are based at Murmansk for the Atlantic and at Petropavlovsk on the Kamchatka Peninsula for the Pacific.[13] Neither base depends on strait passage for exit. The Soviet Navy does not normally station its strategic offensive forces with its Black Sea or Baltic Fleets or with the majority of the Pacific Fleet in the Sea of Japan, where restrictive straits regimes might affect their passage.

Most Soviet surface forces, however, do rely on straits passage to reach the oceans. The Baltic Fleet must pass through the Little Belt, the Great Belt, or the Sound, straits under Danish and Swedish control. For the Little and Great Belts and the Danish side of the Sound, Danish law requires prior notification of passage of warships and surface passage of submarines.[14] Swedish law, for the other side of the Sound, does not require prior notification,[15] but does, in accordance with general principles of international law, require the surface passage of submarines. More restrictive regimes could be instituted in times of war.

The Soviet Black Sea Fleet must pass through the Turkish straits where transit is governed by the 1936 Montreux Convention. The treaty requires prior notification of passage of warships, surface passage of submarines, and single passage (for Black Sea powers, there are stricter rules for non-Black Sea states) of warships heavier than 15,000 tons (e.g., the larger Soviet helicopter cruisers). If Turkey considers herself threatened by war, she may impose more restrictions, though not cut off, warship passage.[16] Due in part to these limitations, Soviet naval forces in the Baltic and Black Sea are largely intended only for neighborhood operations, i.e., in the Baltic and North Sea and in the Black Sea and the Mediterranean.[17] Distant water Atlantic operations are the responsibility of the Northern Fleet, which is unhampered by straits.

In the Pacific, most Soviet surface forces sail out of the Sea of Japan in the region of Vladivastock.[18] Although they can freely transit through the Soviet side of La Perouse Strait, north of Hokkaido, easier access routes are through the straits adjacent to Korea and Japan, which are not now controlled by either coastal state, i.e., through the Korean straits and Tsugaru. The Soviet Navy also shares the transit interests of the United States Navy in the Indonesian straits for passage between the Pacific and Indian Ocean[19] and because of Mediterranean operations by ships from the Northern Fleet shares, to some degree, a concern in free transit through Gibraltar.

These concerns regarding straits explain the attitude of the Soviet Navy. It can be expected to oppose trends in international law restricting naval passage through international straits since it is hemmed in on all sides by straits. More restrictive straits regimes would be more dangerous to the Soviet Navy than to the United States Navy and would put the Soviet fleet in a more disadvantageous position.

Additional problems could afflict the Soviet Navy raised by issues of the second sort, these concerning transit along coasts. 200-mile territorial seas or 200-mile economic zones which had crept to include restrictions on naval passage could restrict the crucial Northern Fleet behind the coastal zones of Britain, Denmark (the Faroe Islands and Greenland), and Iceland, all countries within the NATO alliance. Only the Pacific Fleet from Petropavlovsk and via La Perouse from the Sea of Japan would then have unimpeded access. This situation would radically transform the potential of the Soviet Navy. All the principal Western navies would have free access through their own waters to the Atlantic. The Soviet Navy, on the other hand, would have to pass through NATO territory to reach the Atlantic or would have to send ships from the Pacific Fleet. Obviously, such a development would impair Soviet naval missions. The Soviet Union has already shown considerable displeasure with Norwegian and British offshore oil operations in the North Sea, fearing that drilling platforms will be used for intelligence gear and diminish the effectiveness of the Soviet Northern Fleet.[20]

With this in mind, Gorshkov's reaction to claims for 200-mile seas is not surprising. He supports the "strict establishment of limitations on the breadths of territorial seas," restricting the territorial sea to only 12 miles; otherwise the high seas might be entirely divided up among the coastal states.[21]

Soviet naval opposition to 200-mile territorial seas is not based only on fear about the mobility of the Northern Fleet. As with the United States Navy, the Soviet Navy's naval presence role would be endangered by extensive zones of coastal control. Such activities as the Soviet naval patrol off Ghana to help gain release of Soviet fishing vessels or the Mediterranean buildup to 90 ships as a show of force during the 1973 Arab-Israeli War[22] would be greatly inhibited by 200-mile zones restricting naval passage. Since in terms of both capability and intent the Soviet naval presence role will become more important, it seems likely that the Soviet Navy will continue to oppose restrictions on transit beyond 12 miles for this reason too.

Thus, with regard to straits and transit along coasts, the Soviet Navy has interests very similar to and even greater in intensity than those of the United States Navy, putting it firmly on the side of high seas freedoms. Only in the third area, military use of the seabed, do Soviet and United States naval positions seem to differ. Gorshkov favors the "complete demilitarization of the seabed."[23] This might well be due to a scientific lag, meaning that the Soviet Navy might not have the same capability as the United States Navy to implant and maintain underwater listening devices. On the other hand, this position might be only for propaganda purposes, since in the negotiations leading up to the 1971 Seabed Arms Control Treaty, the Soviet Union switched from the total demilitarization position to join the United States and urge the prohibition only of weapons of mass destruction.[24]

Of all the four major navies examined, the Soviet Navy could lose the most, absolutely and relatively, by the diminution of the freedoms of the high seas. None of the Western navies is in as bad a geographical situation as the Soviet Navy. Now that the Soviet Union has made a very considerable national investment in developing a superpower distant water Navy and since the missions of Soviet sea power could be significantly hampered by restrictions on the freedoms of the high seas, it can be expected that naval interests will play an important part in the formulation of Soviet ocean policy.

The Role of Naval Interests in the Soviet Ocean Policy Process

We have no inside view of the way in which the various Soviet maritime interests promote their positions within the Soviet political system. Little is known about the way in which the Soviet Navy interacts with other government agencies.[25] And, generally, the role of the Soviet military in the making of Soviet foreign policy must only be guessed at.[26] We do know, however, that important foreign policy issues are decided ultimately by the Politburo, under Brezhnev's direction.[27] It is reasonable to assume that the general outline, at least, of ocean policy would be drawn by the Politburo while we must still speculate about the Navy's role in the ocean policy process.

The ocean policy input to the Politburo may well be reflected by the composition of the Soviet delegation to the law of the sea negotiations.[28] Important segments of Soviet maritime opinion should be able to find places in the official delegation in rough proportion to their influence. The head of the Soviet Caracas delegation came from the Ministry of Foreign Affairs. This would tend to indicate that in the Soviet Union, as elsewhere, the foreign ministry coordinates interdepartmental maritime collaborations. Of the nine members of the Soviet delegation, five came from the Ministry of Foreign Affairs, two from the Navy, and one each from the Ministry of Fisheries and the Scientific Research Institute of Maritime Transport. Of nine official advisors, three came from the Ministry of Foreign Affairs, two from the State Committee on Science and Technology, and one each from the Navy, the Ministry of Geology, the Ministry of the Merchant Marine, and the Scientific Research Institute of Maritime Transport. Of these nineteen top Soviet law of the sea representatives, then, Foreign

Affairs had nine delegates, the Navy and merchant marine three each, Science and Technology two, and Fisheries and Geology one each. The composition of the Soviet delegation confirms studies of Soviet ocean activities indicating that the major Soviet maritime interests are the Navy, the merchant marine, fisheries, mineral exploitation, and scientific research.[29]

Considering the nature of the other Soviet interests in the law of the sea, it is likely that the Navy's position in favor of the freedoms of the high seas is supported by most other Soviet maritime interests. Probably Soviet ocean policy is not plagued with so many disputes among maritime interests as is United States ocean policy. The merchant marine is a powerful ocean interest inclined to support the traditional ocean order. The Soviet merchant marine has jumped from 1.8 million deadweight tons in 1950 to 15.0 million deadweight tons in 1972.[30] It is now third in the world in number of ships and seventh in deadweight tonnage.[31] Just as the Soviet Navy might be daunted by restrictive regimes for international straits and along coasts, so might the Soviet merchant marine find itself hemmed in by these same limitations.

It can also be expected that Soviet fisheries interests would side with naval interests. Fish products provide one-third of all animal protein consumed in the Soviet Union and one-fifth of all protein.[32] To catch the fish to supply this protein, the Soviet Union sails the world's largest fishing fleet, which catches the third largest tonnage of fish.[33] Unlike the fishing interests of the United States, which are divided and sometimes neutralized between distant water and coastal groups, Soviet interests are solidly with distant water fishermen since a large proportion of the Soviet catch is taken off the shores of other countries. Again, as a distant water fishing country, the Soviet Union would favor narrow bands of coastal maritime control.

Although Soviet oil and gas development on the continental shelf might call for wider coastal state limits, the Soviet Union's enclosed geographical position would mean that for manganese nodule exploitation the country would have to favor some sort of international access to deep seabed minerals. Mineral exploitation generally seems to have less impact on Soviet policy than on United States policy, though. This is probably because neither offshore drilling nor ocean floor mining is as important or as technologically advanced as in the United States.[34]

Finally, Soviet research activities would favor high seas freedoms. The Soviet Union has developed a considerable oceanological capability for both economic and military purposes.[35] Any extension of coastal state control could limit Soviet research endeavors, since it is unlikely that most states would readily allow foreign research to go unregulated within their maritime zones.

Altogether, then, there seems to be a considerable tilt in the Soviet ocean policy balance toward retention of the traditional system of freedoms of the high seas. There are, doubtless, disputes concerning the exact nature of Soviet law of the sea proposals and the degree to which the Soviet Union should compromise on any given issue. But the probable drift of Soviet ocean policy is clear. The Soviet Union combines great maritime potential with very poor access to the oceans. The United States may be torn between interests in distant water use and interests in coastal use. Considering the composition of United States maritime interests and the geographical position of the country, such division is inevitable. But the Soviet Union is not so favored geographically, and there is a heavy pull by many Soviet maritime interests toward distant water uses and their protection. The Soviet Navy is one of those pulling with the majority.

The Reflection of Naval Interests in Soviet Ocean Policy

The near unanimity of Soviet maritime interests is reflected in the pattern of Soviet ocean policy. The Soviet Union's law of the sea position has remained relatively consistent since the beginning of the seabed debate in the United Nations in 1967. Between 1967 and 1969 the Soviet delegation stressed seabed demilitarization more than it did so subsequently, however. This was largely because discussion dealing with seabed demilitarization shifted from the Seabed Committee to the Conference on the Committee on Disarmament.[36]

On each of the three issues of importance to the Soviet Navy, law of the sea policy has marched to the naval drummer. Given the nature of other Soviet interests, this correlation is not surprising since no influential maritime interests exist that might tug Soviet policy in another direction. Although one cannot conclusively demonstrate that naval interests are the principal concern of Soviet ocean policy, given the importance which the Soviet Union normally gives to security interests, one may conclude that naval interests are second to none.

The Soviet Union has often promoted free transit through international straits.[37] Igor Kolosovsky, the head of the Soviet Caracas delegation, made this declaration, for example, before the Second Committee in 1974:

The security of the USSR depended upon communications by sea and through straits. Consequently, his delegation could not agree that matters relating to navigation through straits admitted unilateral solutions. Attempts to modify the traditional regime or to limit transit through those straits were against the interests of the international community.[38]

The Soviet Union does not consider that innocent passage regimes for international straits would be adequate for its purposes. As Khlestov of the Soviet delegation explained to the Seabed Committee in 1972,

[I]t was hardly possible to claim that a regime of innocent passage would suffice for international straits. Experience in recent years had shown that the regime was sometimes interpreted in different ways; it might result in attempts by States to regulate the passage of ships unilaterally and to obstruct freedom of navigation. In practice, control of those important straits would be in the hands of a small group of States, which would be prejudicial not only to international navigation but also to the entire international community.[39]

This is an ironic reversal of the position the Soviet Union adopted in the First United Nations Conference on the Law of the Sea in Geneva in 1958. Then the Soviet Union sought increased coastal state control as a "sand-in-the-gear-box" technique to restrict Western maritime mobility.[40] The different stance is, of course, a result of the emergence of Soviet maritime capability—naval, fishing, and merchant marine—in the last two decades. Since the beginning of the current law of the sea talks in 1967, the Soviet Union has remained solidly in favor of free passage through straits.

The Soviet Union is acutely aware that restrictions on straits passage would be more damaging to its Navy than to the navies of the West. This awareness surfaced in a presentation by Sapozhnikov of the Ukranian delegation to Caracas's Second Committee in 1974:

Those advocating the principle of control by the coastal state [over straits] based their opinion on the increasing threat represented by the strategic interests of the navies of the super-Powers. It should, however, be clearly stated that the coastal State's control over the straits would not prevent an increase in the number of warships, since most countries possessing such fleets did not have to pass through straits to reach the oceans.[41]

The Soviet Union joined with Bulgaria, Czechoslavakia, East Germany, Poland, and the Ukraine in presenting "Draft Articles on Straits Used for International Navigation" to the Law of the Sea Conference.[42] The basic provision is:

In straits used for international navigation between one part of the high seas and another part of the high seas, all ships in transit shall enjoy the equal freedom of navigation for the purpose of transit passage through such straits.[43]

The draft articles provide that the coastal state may designate transit corridors and that passing ships shall obey international rules concerning the prevention of accidents at sea,[44] but

No State shall be entitled to interrupt or suspend the transit of ships through the straits, or engage therein in any acts which interfere with the transit of ships, or require ships in transit to stop or communicate information of any kind.[45]

This is a radical departure from the rules of innocent passage, because under the draft articles the determination of wrongdoing lies with the flag, not the coastal state, and the coastal state has no power under any conditions to prevent or to delay passage. Unlike innocent passage, too, the draft articles provide for overflight and make no rule insisting on surface passage for submarines.[46]

Because the draft articles make no distinction between straits already under innocent passage regimes and those now with zones of high seas within them, it is possible that the Soviet Union means to extend the right of transit passage to the Danish and Turkish straits. The draft articles state:

In the case of straits leading from the high seas to the territorial sea of one or more foreign States and used for international navigation, the principle of innocent passage for all ships shall apply and this passage shall not be suspended.[47]

Thus, it might be that whether or not the Baltic or Black Seas were considered to be high seas, the Soviet Navy, according to the draft articles, would have a right of passage which "shall not be suspended." This would be a significant improvement on both the regimes of the Danish and Turkish straits for the Soviet Union.

With regard to the second issue of naval interest, coastal transit, the Soviet position has remained firm that territorial seas shall not exceed 12 miles. Even before Malta's Pardo introduced the seabeds to the United Nations in 1967, the Soviet Union was exploring the possibility of convening a new law of the sea conference to settle the unresolved questions of the 1958 and 1960 Geneva conferences. High on the Soviet Union's list of priorities was the limitation of the territorial sea. The Soviet Union was encouraged by indications that the United States might be willing to go along with the Soviet Union and accept the Soviet's traditional maximum of 12 miles.[48] From the earliest meetings of the Seabed Committee, the Soviet Union has stressed the need to limit national claims.[49]

Along with Bulgaria, East Germany, and Poland, the Soviet Union submitted "Draft Articles on the Territorial Sea" for consideration by the Law of the Sea Conference in 1974. These provide for a "maximum limit of 12 nautical miles."[50] As with the draft on straits, the draft on the territorial sea prohibits the coastal state from interfering with the innocent passage of foreign vessels within the territorial sea.[51]

As did the United States, the Soviet Union agreed to accept 200-mile economic zones at Caracas. But also, as did the United States, the Soviet Union made it clear that such an economic zone was strictly contingent upon the preservation of freedoms of the high seas for non-resource uses. Kolosovsky put it this way to the Second Committee at Caracas:

His delegation wished to point out that the granting of sovereign rights in the economic zone to the coastal State was not equivalent to the granting of territorial sovereignty and must in no way interfere with the other lawful activities of States on the high seas, especially with international maritime communications. The Convention must state clearly that the rights of the coastal State in the economic zone must be exercised without prejudice to the rights of any other State recognized in international law.[52]

The new willingness of the Soviet Union to accept 200-mile economic zones in exchange for transit rights is probably a result of the realization that the international pressure for economic zones was too strong to resist. Still, given the importance of Soviet distant-water fishing, the final decision to endanger these operations must have been painful to make. Unlike the United States, the Soviet Union has no good domestic reasons to endorse the 200-mile economic zone. But as long as some part of Soviet fishing activities must be sacrificed, better for the Soviet Union that the sacrifice be recompensed in part, at least, by better protection of naval interests.

On the third naval issue, military use of the deep seabed, the Soviet Union's official policy reflects the Soviet Navy's stated interest in prohibition of all military uses of the ocean floor. As mentioned above, the ardor with which the Soviet Union has pursued this policy objective in the law of the sea negotiations has cooled considerably since the 1960s. A typical statement on seabed demilitarization in the earlier years of the debate is this one from Kulazhenkhov before the First Subcommittee of the Seabed Committee in 1969:

[H]is delegation wished to deal with one of the problems of the sea-bed which it regarded as particularly urgent and pressing. That was the problem of prohibiting the military use of the sea-bed and of creating conditions under which the sea-bed would be used only for peaceful purposes. The success or failure of the efforts to put such a prohibition into effect would decisively influence the development of international co-operation in the exploration and use of the sea-bed. The Soviet Union was in favor of an understanding being reached to prohibit any kind of military use of the sea-bed and ocean floor so that they might be free of military equipment and installations and thus be reserved exclusively for peaceful purposes.[53]

The Soviet Union continues to oppose military activity on the seabed, but it gives the issue far less prominence in its public utterances. In his speech about the deep seabed to the First Committee of the Caracas Conference, for example, Romanov of the Soviet Union devotes only the following few words to the demilitarization point:

The regime must prohibit the use of the sea-bed for military purposes. Otherwise it would contradict the very idea of the common heritage of mankind. The sea-bed must be used exclusively for peaceful purposes.[54]

The reason for this trend might be that the Soviet Union is developing, for itself, the sophisticated technology for using the ocean floor for underwater detection. Another factor might be that the Soviet Union has more to say about the exploitation of the resources of the seabed now and thus has less time to devote to demilitarization. Still another cause might be that the 1971 Seabed Arms Control Treaty solved some of the Soviet Union's problems regarding an ocean-floor arms race. But, insofar as we can understand the positions of the Soviet Navy and the Soviet Union on seabed demilitarization, the two seem to be, once again, in tandem.

Soviet ocean policy, then, is a good reflection of Soviet naval interests, at least of those three issues in which the Soviet Navy has a stake. There do not seem to be the same sort of policy struggles among various maritime interests in the Soviet Union as in the United States: neither would they be predicted by the nature of Soviet maritime interests nor are they seen in the development of public Soviet law of the sea positions. The Soviet Navy's law of the sea preferences are consistently supported by Soviet ocean policy, the most conservative policy among the four naval powers.

Notes

1. S. G. Gorshkov, "Navies in War and in Peace," *Morskoy Sbornik,* 1972–1973, translated in *Naval Institute Proceedings* 100 (November 1974):55–60. For a longer analysis of the Gorshkov piece on ocean law, see Mark W. Janis, "The Soviet Navy and Ocean Law," *Naval War College Review* 26 (March–April 1974):52–58. The authoritative English-language work on traditional Soviet law of the sea policy is William E. Butler, *The Soviet Union and the Law of the Sea* (Baltimore: Johns Hopkins University Press, 1971). The Soviet Union had a less favorable attitude to freedoms of the high seas when its maritime interests were not so great.

2. Gorshkov, "Navies in War and in Peace," *Naval Institute Proceedings* 100 (October 1974):63.

3. Barry M. Blechman, *The Changing Soviet Navy* (Washington: Brookings Institution, 1973), pp. 16–20.

4. John E. Moore (ed.), *Jane's Fighting Ships 1974–1975* (London: Macdonald & Co., 1974), pp. 535–538 and 639.

5. Ibid., p. 642.

6. Blechman, *Soviet Navy,* pp. 16–17.

7. Gorshkov, "Navies in War and in Peace," (October):61–62.

8. Blechman, *Soviet Navy,* pp. 26–29.

9. Gorshkov, "Navies in War and in Peace," (October):59.

10. Ibid.

11. Moore, *Jane's,* p. 532 and 642–643.

12. Gorshkov, "Navies in War and in Peace," (November):58.

13. J. P. Deaton, "The Significance of International Straits to Soviet Naval Operations," March 1975, Naval Postgraduate School, Monterey, California, Master's thesis, pp. 31–32, 47–48, and 111–112.

14. Denmark, "Rules Governing Admittance of Foreign Warships and Military Aircraft to Danish Territory in Peacetime, 25 July 1951," in U.S.S.R., Ministry of Defense, *Manual of International Maritime Law* (Moscow: Military Publishing House, 1966), Naval Intelligence Command Translation No. 2500 (a/b), pp. 312–317.

15. Sweden, "Royal Decree with Respect to the Right of Foreign Warships and Military Aircraft to Call in Swedish Territory in Peacetime, 8 June 1951," in U.S.S.R., *International Maritime Law,* pp. 304–309.

16. Deaton, "International Straits," pp. 55–56.

17. Ibid., pp. 45–46 and 66–68.

18. Ibid., pp. 32–36.

19. Ibid., pp. 85–109.

20. "Norwegian Oil Not for NATO," *Dagens Nyheter* (Stockholm), 3 May 1975, p. 1, in *Foreign Broadcast Information Service,* 8 May 1975, pp. U1–U4. "British Oil Work Worries Russians," *New York Times,* 29 February 1976, p. 17.

21. Gorshkov, "Navies in War and in Peace," (October):58.

22. Mark W. Janis and Donald C. F. Daniel, *The U.S.S.R.: Ocean Use and Ocean Law,* Law of the Sea Institute Occasional Paper No. 21 (Kingston, R.I.: University of Rhode Island, 1974), pp. 2–3.

23. Gorshkov, "Navies in War and in Peace," (November):60.

24. Evan Luard, *The Control of the Sea-Bed* (London: Heinemann, 1974), pp. 104–106.

25. John Erickson, "Soviet Defense Policies and Naval Interests," in M. MccGwire, K. Booth, J. McDonnell (eds.), *Soviet Naval Policy* (New York: Praeger, 1975, p. 59.

26. Malcolm Mackintosh, "The Soviet Military's Influence on Foreign Policy," in *Soviet Naval Policy,* p. 28.

27. Ibid., p. 25.

28. United Nations, General Assembly, *Delegations to the Third United Nations Conference on the Law of the Sea* (A/CONF.62/INF.3), 1974, p. 55.

29. Janis and Daniel, *The U.S.S.R.: Ocean Use and Ocean Law,* p. 1. U.S., Library of Congress, Congressional Research Service, *Soviet Ocean Activities: A Preliminary Survey,* 1975.

30. Center for Strategic and International Studies, *Soviet Sea Power* (Washington: Georgetown University, 1969), p. 81. "Merchant Shipping Data," *Naval Institute Proceedings* 99 (May 1973):364.

31. "Soviet Merchant Marine One of the World's Greatest," TASS (Moscow), 2 December 1972, in U.S., Department of Commerce, Joint Publication Research Service, *U.S.S.R. Political and Sociological Affairs,* No. 313/57824, 1972, p. 15.

32. Center for Strategic and International Studies, *Soviet Sea Power,* p. 94. T. Sealy, "Soviet Fisheries: A Review," *Underwater Journal* 5 (No. 4, 1973):152.

33. Sealy, "Soviet Fisheries," pp. 152, 158, and 173.

34. U.S., Congressional Research Service, *Soviet Ocean Activities,* pp. 55–68.

35. Ibid., pp. 39–46.

36. James A. Barry, Jr., "The Seabed Arms Control Issue: 1967–1971: A Superpower Symbiosis?" *Naval War College Review* 25 (November–December 1972):90.

37. United Nations, General Assembly, *First Committee Records* (A/C.1/PV.1777), 1970, p. 32; *Permanent Sea-Bed Committee Records* (A/AC.138/SR.56), 1971, p. 152, and (A/AC.138/S.C. II/SR.58), 1973, p. 125.

38. United Nations, General Assembly, *Third United Nations Conference on the Law of the Sea* (A/CONF.62/C.2/SR.12), 1974, p. 2.

39. UN, *Permanent Sea-Bed Committee Records* (A/AC.138/SR.83), 1972, p. 71.

40. Arthur H. Dean, "The Geneva Conference on the Law of the Sea: What Was Accomplished," *American Journal of International Law* 52 (October 1958):612.

41. UN, *Law of the Sea Conference* (A/CONF.62/C.2/SR.14), p. 17.

42. Ibid. (A/CONF.62/C.2/L.11).

43. Ibid., p. 1.

44. Ibid., pp. 1–2.

45. Ibid., p. 2.

46. Ibid., pp. 2–3.

47. Ibid., p. 2.

48. John R. Stevenson, "Lawmaking for the Seas," *American Bar Association Journal* 61 (February 1975):187.

49. UN, *Ad Hoc Sea-Bed Committee Records* (A/AC.135/SR.11), 1968, p. 3.

50. UN, *Law of the Sea Conference* (A/CONF.62/C.2/L.26), p. 1.

51. Ibid., p. 3.

52. Ibid. (A.CONF.62/C.2/SR.28), pp. 15–16.

53. UN, *Permanent Sea-Bed Committee Records* (A/AC.138/SC.1/SR.6), 1969, p. 48.

54. UN, *Law of the Sea Conference* (A/CONF.62/C.1/SR.8), p. 8.

3 Great Britain

British Naval Interests in Law of the Sea Issues

Traditional law of the sea was largely the 19th century creation of British sea power. Unrivalled for most of the period 1815 to 1914, the Royal Navy enforced the 3-mile limit and the freedoms of the high seas. Large expanses of high seas served British naval missions well. These missions were to protect Britain's far-flung colonies and trade routes and to project British power ashore throughout Europe and the world. British naval power has diminished considerably since the end of World War II, and there is a strong case to be made that the Royal Navy depends much less heavily on the freedoms of the high seas now than it did before. The new nature of British naval interests in law of the sea issues can be seen against the background of the changing missions and composition of the Royal Navy.

In the past three decades, there has been a significant reduction in the scope of British naval operations. From almost global responsibilities in 1945, the Royal Navy in 1976 is committed principally to regional duties. The current status of British naval missions can be had in the British government's *Statement on the Defence Expenditures 1975,*[1] which outlines three roles for the Royal Navy: maintaining Britain's nuclear deterrent, providing for Britain's and NATO's maritime defense in the Eastern Atlantic and Channel areas, and, to a much lesser extent, protecting British and NATO interests outside the waters around Britain.

With regard to the first naval mission, strategic deterrence, the British declared:

The Polaris force, which Britain will continue to make available to the Alliance, provides a unique European contribution to NATO's strategic nuclear capability out of all proportion to the small fraction of our defence budget which it costs to maintain.[2]

This Polaris force is composed of four SSBNs: *Renown, Repulse, Resolution,* and *Revenge,* each armed with the Polaris A-3 missile with a range of 2500 nautical miles.[3] Although the Chinese are reportedly working on a nuclear-powered ballistic missile submarine,[4] at this point only Britain and France join the superpowers in operating such strategic deterrent boats. The four British SSBNs are the entire part of Britain's strategic deterrent. The deterrent is not viewed in isolation but rather as part of the more powerful NATO deterrent.

The vast majority of Royal naval forces are dedicated to the second mission, regional defense, a mission similar to the United States Navy's sea control role. There are two elements to this second mission: first, providing a flexible, graduated, conventional deterrent to Soviet threats, and, second, serving as a police force for Britain's economic interests in neighboring waters. The first element is again perceived within a NATO framework:

These [the Eastern Atlantic and Channel areas] are the forward sea areas of NATO, corresponding to the Central Region on land, in which NATO's maritime forces face the growing power of the Soviet Navy.

All the sea-borne supply and reinforcement routes from North America to Britain and the European mainland pass through these areas. If the balance of maritime power were allowed to shift so far in favour of the Warsaw Pact that it had an evident ability in a period of tension to isolate Europe by sea, the effect on Allied confidence and political cohesion would be profound.

NATO depends critically on Britain to provide the main weight of the maritime forces immediately available to the Alliance in these areas; it is for this reason that the Government plans to maintain its contribution to the defence of these areas virtually undiminished.[5]

Some voices in the United Kingdom insist that the Royal Navy should make defense of British fishing and offshore oil exploitation a separate naval mission.[6] The Royal Navy has been reluctant to admit that this is a distinguishable role, instead insisting that these police activities can be carried out with the forces already provided for NATO.[7] This seems to be the attitude of the British government as well.[8] Great Britain has no special coast guard of its own, and there is naval reluctance to have the Royal Navy abandon some of or all its distant-water missions to assume a coast guard identity. Still, with the expansion of offshore drilling and the likely extension of British fishing waters, this second element of the Royal Navy's regional defense role is likely to take on greater importance. A sign of this development is that Britain is now building five naval vessels especially to protect North Sea oil operations.[9] The Soviet Union is reportedly "paranoic" about Britain's offshore oil installations, fearing that they will be used to monitor the Soviet Navy, and has sent intelligence ships so dangerously close to the oil rigs that the Royal Navy has had to be called in to chase them away.[10]

The third British naval mission, protecting distant water interests, is much less important than it once was and is continuing to diminish in significance. The 1975 *Statement* committed Great Britain to withdrawing the Royal Navy from the Mediterranean other than Gilbraltar, leaving only relatively minor distant commitments in Hong Kong, Belize, and the Falkland Islands and with little actual force to support these.[11] Although it is the British intent to deploy the Navy outside the Eastern Atlantic and Channel areas "from time to time,"[12] "commitments outside the NATO area were of lowest priority in strictly military terms."[13] Before a Subcommittee of the Expenditure Committee of the House of Commons, the Ministry of Defence admitted that "the Navy, on its own, would be in no position to defend British merchant shipping outside NATO waters."[14] "Almost all Royal Naval vessels, wherever deployed, are earmarked for assignment in one of three NATO naval categories."[15]

Comparing the missions of the Royal Navy to those of the United States and Soviet navies, one notes that the Royal Navy shares, albeit to a lesser degree, the strategic deterrence role. Like the United States Navy, the Royal Navy has a sea control role, but it is only for regional waters and is also similar to the Soviet Navy's conventional defense of the homeland mission. Although the Royal Navy, like the United States Navy today, once had a considerable projection of power ashore role, this is now much diminished. Finally, Britain seems to give far less prominence to the naval presence mission than either the United States or the Soviet Union.

To carry out its missions, the Royal Navy is, despite slippage, still the world's third most powerful fleet.[16] Besides its Polaris forces, the United Kingdom sails an aircraft carrier, two helicopter carriers, about 75 major surface combatants, and about 450 other surface ships.[17] There are also 8 nuclear-powered fleet submarines and 23 diesel-powered patrol submarines.[18] These forces give Britain significant regional naval power able both to make a graduated response to Soviet pressure and to protect Britain's economic interest. The Royal Navy is also certainly capable of making shows of force in other areas.

From the standpoint of British naval missions and the geography of the region, it would seem that British naval interests should be less in favor of freedoms of the high seas than the interests of either the United States or the Soviet Union. The strategic deterrence mission does not require access through straits or along coasts of other states. Great Britain has clear underwater sailing to the Atlantic. Insofar as restrictive regimes might limit Soviet antisubmarine operations, the British deterrent is safer with extended spheres of national sovereignty than with the traditional freedoms of the high seas. Similarly, regional defense might be facilitated by restrictions on the Soviet Navy whereas limitations on navigation rights would not hinder the Royal Navy in either its regional contribution to NATO or its policing function. Given that naval operations in the Mediterranean and Indian Ocean will be of diminishing importance for the Royal Navy, straits passage is becoming a less and less significant concern.

But one should not conclude that the Royal Navy is, in fact, promoting new zones of coastal state sovereignty. Rather, it seems that the Royal Navy, like the United States and Soviet navies, remains in favor of traditional freedoms of the high seas. The explanation for this naval position must be found outside the context of British naval missions.

There seem to be four reasons for Royal naval support for high seas freedoms. First, the Royal Navy has so long a tradition of maintaining the freedoms of the high seas that it is difficult for the Navy to change its attitude. Second, because the Royal Navy and Great Britain are so thoroughly committed to the NATO alliance, the Royal Navy supports free navigation rights to promote the perceived interests of the United States Navy. Third, although theoretically the Soviet Navy might be boxed in behind extended coastal zones, there is fear that the Soviet Navy would resist any such attempt, and thus great friction and the possibility of conflict would result. Fourth (this is considered at length in the next section), other British maritime interests are inclined toward the protection of freedoms of the high seas and reinforce the Royal Navy's leanings.

Although these four are all good reasons for continued naval support for freedoms of the high seas, one suspects that the possible benefits of increased coastal state jurisdictions for British naval missions have not been fully appreciated. The Royal Navy, even more than the United States Navy, might consider the relative advantages of a new ocean regime for the accomplishment of naval objectives. This point is more thoroughly discussed in Chapter 7. At this juncture, let us turn to the participation of the Royal Navy in the British ocean policy process.

The Role of Naval Interests in the British Ocean Policy Process

The British ocean policy process, while not so shrouded in secrecy as the process in the Soviet Union, is much less publicized than that in the United States. The British ocean policy process shares a tradition of privacy with British executive decision making in general. Probably many American government bureaucrats envy the comfortable distance their British counterparts put between themselves and those curious-to-know. Furthermore, compared with the United States, there is less legislative input into the ocean policy process.

Given that most British ocean policy is formulated well within the world of Whitehall, the Royal Navy is well situated to make a considerable impact on the development of British law of the sea positions. Naval representatives are normally included in the private web of committees that coordinate and compromise the various interests of the different bureaucracies. The Royal Navy is a steady participant in the committees dealing with ocean policy, its interests being forwarded both by naval officers assigned to the Ministry of Defence and by civilians in MOD's Defence Secretariat No. 5, which is charged with some aspects of naval policy planning as well as with international law questions. Of the twenty-nine representatives and alternates whom the United Kingdom sent to Caracas, seven came from the Ministry of Defence, a total surpassed only by the nine attached to the Foreign Office or to another diplomatic function.[19] The Foreign Office has the responsibility of leading the British delegation to the law of the sea negotiations.

The Royal Navy's position in favor of freedoms of the high seas finds support not only from the Foreign Office, but, importantly, from the Department of Trade. Unlike the United States or the Soviet Union, the United Kingdom often ranks merchant shipping interests highest when listing national interests to be advanced by national ocean policy.[20] David Ennals, Britain's Minister of State for Foreign and Commonwealth Affairs, presented shipping's case to the Caracas Conference:

As an island nation, the United Kingdom had always had a special interest in the sea, which had at times isolated it, but had also been its link with the rest of the world. Britain lived by trade, and 98.5 per cent of its trade, by weight, was sea-borne. Much of the trade—oil, raw materials and food—was shipped over long distances. If sea transport were to be less dependable or became more expensive, his country's economy would be harmed more than those of continental or more self-sufficient countries.[21]

Not only is Great Britain's reliance on shipping greater than that of the United States and the Soviet Union, but the United Kingdom is less able to protect it. The shipping interests are vitally concerned with unhindered transit rights protected by an internationally agreed-to treaty.[22] Without transit rights through straits and along coasts, merchant shipping might become less dependable and more expensive. And without an international treaty, it would be difficult to assert Britain's commercial passage rights in the face of coastal state opposition.

Merchant shipping, the Royal Navy, the Foreign Office, and general considerations of the long British tradition favoring freedoms of the high seas all push the United Kingdom toward a conservative, traditional law of the sea position. Increasingly, however, there is countervailing pressure. Fishing interests have shifted from a stand of uniformly favoring freedoms of the high seas to one advocating an international agreement for 200-mile national fishing zones.[23] Throughout the 1972–1973 Anglo-Icelandic Cod War, the fishing groups demanded narrow coastal state jurisdictions.[24] Now a combination of factors, including the realization that a 200-mile fishing zone excluding foreign fishermen would give British fishermen a large profitable fishing area, have prompted fishing interests to unite for increased national limits. In the new Cod War beginning in 1975, British fishermen no longer oppose broad jurisdictions generally, but they do oppose the extension of Iceland's zone before 200-mile fishing limits are adopted by the Law of the Sea Conference.[25] According to the regulations of the European Economic Community, Great Britain would have to share its 200-mile economic zone with its eight European partners and would have the right to share their zones.[26] British fishermen, however, seek to preserve a 100-mile zone exclusively for themselves, leaving the outer 100 miles for EEC fishing waters.[27]

Fishing interests are joined by oil and gas interests that wish to see reliable systems of national control over continental shelf resources.[28] The energy crisis and the importance of North Sea oil have made these interests increasingly influential. The British government has also contributed to an international consortium for the exploitation of manganese nodules from the deep seabed,[29] but the hard-rock interests seems to be much less influential in Great Britain than in the United States. Pollution control, however, is a significant factor joining in the pull for increased coastal state regulation.[30]

Increasingly, public attention is being turned to the advantages of a change in British ocean policy. The *Guardian,* for example, published:

[The] fundamental objective must be to establish an active claim, as an island nation, to all the resources of our continental shelf—the fish as well as the oil.[31]

And the Fabians have argued against British support for freedoms of the high seas and encouraged extended zones of national or regional jurisdiction:

Although the freedom of safe navigation should certainly continue to be protected, the interests both of the British people and of the international community at large now require that a system of planned sea use should be substituted for the present laissez-faire, which is wasteful, dangerous and unjust.[32]

British ocean policy, as presented in the next section, shows some signs, as does United States policy, of the increasing influence of coastal interests. It may be that within Whitehall much the same sort of battle as in the United States is raging, with the Royal Navy, like the United States Navy, standing for freedoms of the high seas. But there might be two significant differences. First, the interests of the Royal Navy are even less clearly on the side of high sea freedoms than those of the United States Navy. The naval determination to protect transit rights is probably not so fervent. Second, the importance of the merchant marine is much greater in Britain than in the United States. One expects that commercial interests are bearing the burden of defending the freedoms of the high seas, a burden borne by the Navy in the United States. Both of these differences tend to make the political situation of the Royal Navy less critical in British ocean policy making than that of the United States Navy in United States policy making. The Royal Navy is in more of a supporting role.

The Reflection of Naval Interests in British Ocean Policy

The Royal Navy's perceived interests in freedoms of the high seas is reflected in British ocean policy. The Royal Navy's impact, however, seems relatively less significant than that of either the United States Navy or the Soviet Navy. At the Law of the Sea Conference Ennals did include naval interests among those which the United Kingdom would attempt to protect:

[H]is country had defence commitments which must not be imperilled. It was concerned not only with the defence of British interests, but with the fulfillment of its obligations to other nations in the areas of the Mediterranean and the North Atlantic, the Persian Gulf, the Indian Ocean and the Pacific. Those interests, like those of other countries, required the freedom of navigation and overflight.[33]

The place of defense interests is important to note. In this speech, not untypically, Ennals put defense fifth in a list of seven British maritime interests: after the merchant marine, offshore oil, deep-sea minerals, and fishing, and ahead of scientific research and pollution. Speeches of the United States and Soviet delegations would commonly put defense nearer the top of any list. Furthermore, unlike the United States and Soviet Union, Great Britain does not insist that transit rights for naval vessels are the absolutely essential element in a law of the sea package. Rather, the protection of naval interests is only part of a preferable solution of ocean policy problems. This difference in stress is an important distinction between British law of the sea policy and that of the superpowers.

Despite the difference in emphasis, there are striking similarities in the details of the proposals of Britain and those of the United States and Soviet Union. The British position on straits and territorial seas was elaborated in their 1974 "Draft Articles on the Territorial Sea and Straits."[34] Chapter 3 of these articles provides that "all ships and aircraft enjoy the right of transit passage, which shall not be impeded."[35] The right of transit passage applies to any strait which:

(a) is used for international navigation;
(b) connects two parts of the high seas.

    Transit passage shall apply in a strait only to the extent that:

(a) an equally suitable high seas route does not exist through the strait; or
(b) if the strait is formed by an island of the coastal State, an equally suitable high seas passage does not exist seaward of the island.[36]

There are no special provisions for warships. Naval passage would be outside the discretion of the coastal state which "shall not hamper transit passage."[37] And, although the coastal state may provide for sea lanes and traffic separation schemes,[38] regulations concerning safety procedures and pollution are to be "generally accepted international regulations,"[39] not rules independently established by the straits state.

With regard to passage through territorial seas, the British draft articles concede coastal state control over security determinations for the innocent passage of warships,[40] but they also firmly fix the limits of the territorial sea at no more than 12 miles.[41] In debating the proposed 200-mile economic zone, the British delegation has insisted, along with the United States and the Soviet Union, that beyond 12 miles traditional rights of free navigation should persist.[42]

The United Kingdom's position on straits and coastal zones does, of course, accommodate the Royal Navy's perceived interests. But, at least equally importantly, the British stand also protects shipping interests. Sir Roger Jackling, the Permanent Leader of the British law of the sea delegation, stressed the interests of the merchant marine at Caracas, arguing that there had to be the maximum freedom for world shipping and that coastal state regulations could impair world trade by the prescription of differing standards for ship construction:

At present shipbuilders knew the standard of construction they had to adopt to meet internationally agreed discharge regulations, but if they were faced with a series of varying regulations, it would be virtually impossible to design ships that could move through all the areas that were regulated. Consequently the economy of ship movement would be drastically reduced and the cost of world trade significantly increased.[43]

Neither the United States nor the Soviet Union devotes a corresponding degree of attention to the possible plight of merchant shipping. The British free transit position may well be a result more of shipping than of naval interests. But the British draft articles cannot be attributed solely to concern for the merchant marine. It would be considerably easier to obtain international agreement on free passage for merchant vessels unconnected to free passage for warships. As Chapter 5 shows, many more states favor free transit for commercial ships than favor free transit for military vessels. Even the regime of innocent passage could well be sufficiently generous to allow for the unimpeded transit of commercial shipping. The restrictions of innocent passage concern submerged passage, overflight, and the determination of security, all of which limit naval operations much more than commercial ones. If Britain were attempting to protect merchant shipping with no regard for naval shipping, it would be strongly tempted to call only for the preservation of innocent passage rights as long as such were unhindered by new coastal state environmental powers. It seems that Great Britain is making the merchant marine position more tenuous by linking it to naval interests. There must be, then, a special British willingness to promote naval concerns independent of any commercial shipping interest.

Another indication of the importance of naval interests is that Great Britain has refused to claim a 200-mile economic zone despite the push of fishing and mineral interests. This determination to wait for a settlement at the Law of the Sea Conference instead of proceeding unilaterally can be attributed to the same fear that restrained the United States—that a declaration of 200-mile economic zones will prompt other states to do the same or more. But given the existing rules of innocent passage, such 200-mile zones would not be very dangerous for commercial shipping but might significantly endanger naval operations. Once again, it appears that a naval, not a merchant marine, interest is at stake.

But one must be careful not to put protection of naval mobility as high on the British list as on the lists of the United States and the Soviet Union. Not only are British naval interests very different nowadays, but Great Britain must be more pliable in the law of the sea negotiations than either of the superpowers. Britain relies more heavily on the sea for trade and for security than either the United States or the Soviet Union, but Britain no longer has the sea power to ensure a favorable ocean regime, sea power which it had in the 19th century. The United States and the Soviet Union can both threaten to "go it alone" without a law of the sea treaty, continuing to make use of the oceans and protecting their uses with naval power. This is not the best alternative, but it is a possibility. It is not such a realistic alternative for Great Britain. Britain can protect shipping better than most, but it does not have the strength that it once had or that the superpowers have now, and it must rely considerably on coastal state consent for the passage of its merchant traders. Furthermore, as a country with large coastal interests in offshore oil, fisheries, and pollution, it has real concern to establish effective management of coastal zone activities. Such management will be much more difficult if no law of the sea treaty is reached. Great Britain would not, for example, prefer to play Iceland to Russia's Britain in an Anglo-Russian fish war about a unilaterally declared 200-mile British fisheries zone.

This combination of significant distant-water trading interests and coastal management interests along with the diminishing British sea power makes the United Kingdom especially willing to compromise, in order to devise a law of the sea convention with broad backing from many nations. Some Britishers say that, because of the United Kingdom's mix of interests, if only the United Nations would let Great Britain write the new rules for the law of the sea, everyone would be happy. Faintly reminiscent of both 19th century British liberal political philosophy and 19th century British-imposed law of the sea, this solution is unlikely today. Britain's ships no longer rule the waves, but must flow with the current.

Notes

1. Great Britain, Secretary of State for Defence, *Statement on the Defence Estimates 1975.*

2. Ibid., p. 10.

3. John E. Moore (ed.), *Jane's Fighting Ships 1974–1975* (London: Macdonald & Co., 1974), p. 348.

4. Ibid., p. 78.

5. Great Britain, *Defence Estimates,* pp. 9–10.

6. Royal Naval College, *Papers and Discussions at the Greenwich Forum Conference "Exploitation of the North Sea"* (Greenwich, London: n.p., 1975), pp. 58 and 75–76.

7. Ibid., pp. 86–87.

8. Ibid., pp. 92–93.

9. "British Oil Work Worries Russians," *New York Times,* 29 February 1976, p. 17.

10. Ibid.

11. Great Britain, *Defence Estimates,* pp. 13–15.

12. Ibid., p. 15.

13. Great Britain, Parliament, *Second Report from the Expenditure Committee: The Defence Review Proposals 1975* (Commons), p. ix.

14. Ibid., p. xii.

15. Ibid., p. x.

16. Gordon Lee, *Sea Power: The Royal Navy* (London: The Economist, 1973), p. 8.

17. Moore (ed.), *Jane's,* pp. 330 and 642–643.

18. Ibid, pp. 349–351 and 642.

19. United Nations, General Assembly, *Delegations to the Third Law of the Sea Conference* (A/CONF.62/INF.3), 1974, pp. 56–57.

20. Great Britain, Foreign and Commonwealth Office, *The Third United Nations Law of the Sea Conference: Consultations with Non-Governmental Organisations and Individuals on British Policy at the Conference 1974,* pp. 2–3.

21. United Nations, General Assembly, *The Third Law of the Sea Conference* (A/CONF.62/SR.29), 1974, p. 5.

22. Great Britain, *Consultations 1974,* p. 22.

23. Ibid., pp. 6, 8, 11, and 13.

24. "Yes, we have a cod war," *Economist,* 19 September 1972, p. 71. "War in the northern seas," *Economist,* 19 May 1973, p. 104. R. B. Bilder, "The Anglo-Icelandic Fisheries Dispute," *Wisconsin Law Review* 1973:123.

25. "Navy goes in to aid trawlers" and "Zone Goal," *Manchester Guardian Weekly,* November 30, 1975, p. 3.

26. Mark W. Janis, "The Development of European Regional Law of the Sea," *Ocean Development and International Law* 1 (Fall 1973):278–282.

27. "EEC plan for fish limits," *Manchester Guardian Weekly* (London), 1 February 1976, p. 3.

28. Great Britain, Foreign and Commonwealth Office, *The Third United Nations Law of the Sea Conference: Consultations with Non-Governmental Organisations and Individuals on British Policy at the Conference 1975*, p. 14.

29. Great Britain, *Consultations 1974*, p. 18.

30. Great Britain, *Consultations 1975*, p. 18.

31. "Britannia to rule more waves," *Manchester Guardian Weekly* (London), 8 February 1975, p. 18.

32. Elizabeth Young and Brian Johnson, *The Law of the Sea*, Fabian Research Series No. 313 (London: The Fabian Society, 1973), p. 44. Also, on coastal zone management for Britain nationally or regionally, see Elizabeth Young and Peter Fricke (eds.), *Sea Use Planning*, Fabian Tract No. 437 (London: The Fabian Society, 1975). For a conservative view of the same, see Laurance Reed, *Ocean-Space: Europe's New Frontier* (London: Bow Publications, 1969).

33. UN, *Law of the Sea Conference* (A/CONF.62/SR.29), p. 8.

34. Ibid. (A/CONF.62/C.2/L.3).

35. Ibid., p. 8.

36. Ibid.

37. Ibid., p. 10.

38. Ibid., p. 9.

39. Ibid., p. 8.

40. Ibid., pp. 2–3.

41. Ibid., p. 2.

42. Ibid. (A/CONF.62/C.2/SR.25), p. 18.

43. Ibid., p. 20.

4 France

French Naval Interests in Law of the Sea Issues

The French Navy currently holds fourth place among the navies of the world, and naval developments in France are so strong as to leave "little doubt" that in a decade the French Navy will take the third position from the British.[1] French naval interests in the law of the sea debate can be seen from the perspective of the roles of the French Navy as authoritatively defined in the *Livre Blanc sur la Défense Nationale* (White Book on National Defense) published in two volumes in 1972 and 1973 by the French Ministry of Defense.[2] The *Livre Blanc* remains the indispensible source for any study of the French military and its mission structure.[3] The *Livre Blanc* provides three objectives for the armed forces generally: the territorial security of France, the security of Europe and the Mediterranean, and the fulfillment of France's overseas commitments. The responsibilities and composition of the French Navy will be surveyed briefly before turning to the French Navy's maritime legal interests.

The crucial element, as perceived by the French government, in ensuring the territorial security of France is an independent retaliatory capacity.[4] The way in which France can remain independent from the United States yet still protected from the Soviet Union is a subject of intense and continuing debate.[5] Although not all theorists agree, the French government insists that an independent defense must be based on possession of nuclear weapons.[6] France's nuclear arsenal is intended to provide first for the territorial security of France and second for the defense of Europe and the Mediterranean.[7]

The *Livre Blanc* notes the need for France to maintain a three-pronged nuclear potential: airborne nuclear weapons, land-based missiles with nuclear warheads, and SSBNs.[8] Unlike the United Kingdom, which relies on SSBNs alone, France resembles a mini-superpower with all three capabilities. The French Navy has an important role in providing the SSBN part of the French nuclear deterrent. Five nuclear-powered ballistic missile submarines have been built, and all but the last are now operational: *Le Redoutable, Le Terrible, Le Foudroyant, L'Indomptable,* and *Le Tonnant.*[9] The boats are armed with the M-1 missile with a 1400-mile range but the last three vessels will have the M-2 missile with an 1875-mile range. Work is proceeding on an M-4 missile with a 3000-mile range. Great Britain's SSBN force relies heavily on United States technology, but the French have developed their SSBN arm on an independent basis free of aids or transfers from the superpowers.[10] During the next decade, the relative importance of the French Navy's nuclear contribution will increase, becoming the crucial aspect of France's deterrent. The Mirage IV bombers armed with nuclear weapons will probably be all phased out by this time,[11] and it is generally accepted that France's SSBN force is more secure than France's few land-based nuclear warhead missiles.[12] In 1972, when the French government announced the missions assigned to the French Navy to be accomplished by 1985, the priority duty was the creation of a nuclear deterrent capacity.[13]

The French Navy is also expected to protect France's maritime approaches, a mission which fits within the first category of the *Livre Blanc,* territorial security. Conventional defense forces are meant to provide a threshold to test an enemy's convictions before launching a nuclear attack.[14] French conventional naval forces are, however, meant to be more than merely threshold devices. The Navy has important obligations regarding France's overseas commitments, since naval forces are expected to give France the capability of intervening abroad to aid friendly regimes.[15] Furthermore, the Navy is expected to have a blue-water capability for protecting sea lanes vital for French trade and communication.[16] Interestingly, the French, like the Americans and the Russians, stress the importance of naval forces as a "presence":

In times of peace as in times of crisis the Navy permits the government, by a mere demonstration of its presence in the Mediterranean, the Atlantic, and elsewhere to affirm its freedom of action or mediation.[17]

Although the French use neither our terminology nor our categories, it can be seen that the expressed missions of the French

Navy are nearly the same as those of the United States Navy: nuclear deterrence, sea control, projection of power ashore, and naval presence. To carry out their duties, in addition to the 5 SSBNs, the French Navy sails 2 aircraft carriers, 51 surface combatants (2 cruisers, 22 destroyers, and 27 frigates), 19 patrol submarines, and about 250 other vessels.[18] These are largely up-to-date and professional ships.[19] As with their SSBN fleet, the French pride themselves that their naval fleet is built and maintained independently.[20]

The interests of French sea power in law of the sea issues are, as for the Royal Navy, curiously complex. Insofar as the French view themselves as a great maritime power with the desire and potential to intervene abroad, French naval interests are clearly for freedoms of the high seas. But insofar as the French see the Navy's role as defensive against the Soviet Union, French naval interests incline toward extended zones of coastal state sovereignty. The analysis of French naval interests in the law of the sea is simplified by France's insistence on playing the part of a great power. In 1970, for example, the Minister of Defense rejoiced that the high seas were "at one time the domain of the independence and of the power" of states.[21]

Certainly, relative to most other states, especially those in Africa or Asia, French naval power is sufficiently great to enable France to consider herself a relatively influential power. French capacity to intervene, French ability to defend sea lanes against small-power interference, is not inconsiderable. However, relative to the superpowers, French naval potential is not great. The Royal Navy may incline to high seas freedoms in part to back up the valuable American ally, but probably this is not a crucial factor for French sentiment. France visualizes the French Navy as independent of both United States and Soviet forces. Given this French independence, it is questionable that either French security or the French contribution to European and Mediterranean security is enhanced by narrow bands of coastal state control. For example, 200-mile seas would engulf the Mediterranean, perhaps even make it a regional "lake." Both Soviet and United States access would be much more difficult, and the relative weight of French naval force in the region would be appreciated. One wonders, given France's naval strength and the relative importance of territorial security and regional security versus the goal of fulfilling commitments abroad, why French sea power interests should not be in favor of restricting naval access.

The simple answer is that French naval interests are defined to be on the side of high seas freedoms because of French pride. France is proud of the Navy and proud of France's historical role as an influential world power. French naval interests are seen to be those of a naval power, and since naval powers want to send their navies where they please, high seas freedoms are necessary. But there are some more substantial reasons as well. The straits of Gibraltar are the vital connecting link between the Atlantic and the Mediterranean and between France's two major naval contingents. Control of Gibraltar by Spain and Morocco would not only threaten French naval mobility but thereby give both countries greater political leverage vis-à-vis France. Even if 200-mile zones did make the Mediterranean a regional lake, there are no assurances that coastal states would be happier with a French naval presence than with a Russian or American one. France does relish its overseas commitments (considerably more than Great Britain), and sacrificing naval access in areas such as the South Atlantic and the Indian Ocean would be felt as a real loss. Finally, French maritime trade is considerable, and sea lanes are worth protecting with the presence of French naval forces.[22]

These advantages of high seas freedoms must be weighed against the advantages which other powerful navies gain from easy ocean access. Despite its diversity, the French nuclear capacity is not great. It may be easier for a potential enemy to track the two or three French SSBNs out at sea at one time than to track 10 times that number, and France does have to worry about Soviet antisubmarine warfare operations.[23] Extended seas would put France's threshold forces further from the coast in times of crisis, giving them even greater depth with which to test an enemy's intentions. And, as mentioned before, the possible limitations on Soviet and United States Mediterranean operations by restrictions on straits and coastal passage must be a temptation for French naval interests.

As with the British, the French perceive their naval interests to rest with the preservation of the freedoms of the high seas. This analysis only suggests the relative advantages of greater coastal state control for French naval interests. The French naval input to French ocean policy making inclines to that position taken by the navies in the United States, the Soviet Union, and Great Britain.

The Role of Naval Interests in the French Ocean
Policy Process

Although the French ocean policy process is not itself a subject of scholarly debate, there is considerable interest in France in the law of the sea and in maritime questions generally.[24] Actual law of the sea negotiations are in the hands of the French Foreign Ministry, personnel from which have served as president, vice president, secretary general, and assistant secretary general in the French law of the sea delegation.[25] Of thirteen counselors to the delegation, five also came from the Foreign Ministry, three from the Navy, two from the merchant marine, and one each from the Cultural and Environmental Ministry, the Ministry of Industry, Commerce and Arts, and the National Center for the Exploitation of the Oceans. Two academic international lawyers served as legal advisors.

The composition of the French delegation reflects the various French maritime interests. Most of these tend to favor the high seas freedom position of the Navy, a position clearly stated by a high-ranking officer on the Naval Staff, the former commander of the French aircraft carrier, *Clemenceau,* Antoine Sanguinetti:

Several states have already unilaterally appropriated an immense coastal zone and consider it as their territorial sea. France among others has refused to accept such pretensions. But several states, going even further, seek to ensure that future conventions fetter the movements of warships and certain other specialized vessels in this zone of 200 miles and in straits.

These serious attacks on the traditional liberties of the high seas and on the international status of the oceans will only, contrary to the wishes of their promoters, lead to a worsening of tensions, incidents, and conflicts, for which we must ineluctably prepare ourselves.[26]

The French naval attitude favoring the freedoms of the high seas is seconded by the next most influential interest in the development of French ocean policy, the merchant marine. France is the third largest exporting state in the world.[27] Some 60 percent of France's foreign trade is carried by sea.[28] France's dependence on maritime commerce is, however, considerably greater than the size of the French merchant marine. Only 18 percent of French maritime trade is carried aboard French vessels. The French merchant marine constitutes only 1.5 percent of the world's total merchant shipping, and France has only 10 percent as many vessels as Japan, only 25 percent as many as Britain, and only 50 percent as many as Italy.[29] The dependence of France on foreign merchant shipping only strengthens the French preference for freedom of navigation. Since France is already overly reliant on foreign shippers, new dependence on the keepers of important straits and coasts for commercial access would only increase France's maritime vulnerability.

Another important ocean interest, the French scientific research program, would also be threatened by the extension of coastal state control. The French oceanography effort is one of the world's greatest.[30] There are some eleven different government agencies all involved in oceanological studies.[31]

French fishermen are less modernized than many of their competitors,[32] and the European Economic Community has already opened French fishing waters to more efficient German, Dutch, and Belgian fleets.[33] The potential for offshore oil and gas is less in France than elsewhere.[34] Thus, fishing and oil and gas, two interests which are important influences for extended coastal zones in the United States and the United Kingdom, are rather less crucial in the development of French ocean policy.

There is, therefore, a relative harmony of French maritime interests. The naval preference for freedoms of the high seas is supported by other French ocean concerns. As would be expected, this harmony is reflected in French ocean policy.

The Reflection of Naval Interests in French Ocean Policy

The French position in the law of the sea negotiations reflects the Navy's preference for navigation rights and is similar to the positions taken by the other naval powers. The vice president of the French delegation, Roger Jeannel, put the case for 12-mile territorial seas and free transit through straits first in his issue-by-issue presentation at Caracas:

His country had come out in favour of a limit of 12 nautical miles from the baselines, which seemed sufficient to safeguard the security of the coastal States while protecting the interests of international society. A territorial sea of 12 miles seemed the largest area over which the coastal State could exercise the control essential to its sovereignty. That sovereignty would remain subject to the right of innocent passage as traditionally defined. However, since the right could be suspended and the determination of the innocent nature of the passage left partly to the discretion of the coastal State, it was not sufficient for the protection of the interests of other States in straits used for international navigation. Such straits must therefore be covered by a right of free transit not dependent on the coastal States.[35]

The French accepted, as did the Americans, the Russians, and the British, a 200-mile economic zone at the outset of the Caracas Conference in 1974. As with the other maritime powers, the French made clear that the 200-mile zone was not to infringe the rights of passage. But more so than the other maritime powers, the French attempted to present this position as an effort to compromise opposing interests.[36] Jeannel explained that the developing countries really sought only economic gain from the 200-mile zone and that it was possible to have full rights to the resources without having general ownership in the area. He drew upon the rules of French domestic law as an analogy.[37] Jeannel argued that the law of the flag state, not the coastal state, must regulate vessels passing through the economic zone:

The law of the flag State was the only guarantee of freedom of movement since it forbade the interference of any warship or police vessel with the movement of any ship not flying its flag. Although that law had been devised by the maritime Powers, it actually protected the weak against those few which alone had the material means to police the sea.[38]

Although the French rationale is more courteous to the developing states, the position is ultimately the same as that of the other naval powers: a 200-mile economic zone is acceptable but only as long as transit is assured. The French insistence on transit rights through straits and along coasts has a substantial foundation in French sea power interests. In 1971, Michel Debré, the French Minister of Defence, made an exception to the need for maintaining an independent policy line when it came to matters concerning maritime mobility:

On the sea the situation is more flexible than on land; there the protection of our national interests, in particular maintenance of our freedom of movement in the Atlantic and the Mediterranean, has much to gain from cooperation with interests similar to ours.[39]

Debré's statement has two interesting aspects. Not only does it show France's perceived defense interest in free navigation, but it demonstrates that the French view the law of the sea negotiations as an area where cooperation with other nations with similar interest, i.e., the naval powers, is permissible. Given the French desire to be seen as a great power and the consequent decision to act as if France were a great power, France assumes that what is good for sea powers must be good for France. In this fashion, despite the usual policy of independence vis-à-vis the superpowers pursued by France, French ocean policy promotes not only perceived French naval interests but the naval interests of the other maritime powers.

France has imitated the superpowers both in terms of naval mission and composition and in its law of the sea positions. France attempts to look like and sound like an important and independent naval power. While one cannot quarrel with the French Navy's relative importance, one wonders if the French Navy's independent capability vis-à-vis the superpowers is sufficiently great to warrant French support for legal propositions favoring naval mobility.

Notes

1. J. E. Moore, "France and Her Navy," *Navy International* 79 (No. 11, 1974):10.

2. France, Ministre d'État chargé de la Défense Nationale, *Livre Blanc sur la Défense Nationale,* vol. 1 (1972), vol. 2 (1973).

3. Guy Brossollet, *Essai sur la non-bataille* (Paris: Editions Belin, 1975), p. 12.

4. France, Ambassade, Service de presse et d'information, "Valery Giscard d'Estaing, Broadcast over French Television, March 25, 1975," pp. 1–3.

5. Maurice Bertrand, *Pour une doctrine militaire française* (Paris: Gallimard, 1965). Raoul Girardet, *Problèmes Contemporains de Défense Nationale* (Paris: Dalloz, 1974). Brossollet, *Essai sur la non-bataille.* Antoine Sanguinetti, *Le fracas des armes* (Paris: Hachette, 1975).

6. France, "Giscard d'Estaing, March 25, 1975," p. 2.

7. France, *Livre Blanc,* vol. 1, p. 6.

8. Ibid., pp. 12–13.

9. John E. Moore (ed.), *Jane's Fighting Ships 1974–1975* (London: Macdonald & Co., 1974), p. 121.

10. Henri le Masson, "The French Navy—Today and Tomorrow," *Navy International* 77 (No. 10, 1972):14.

11. Brossollet, *Essai sur la non-bataille,* p. 21.

12. Sanguinetti, *Le fracas des armes,* p. 24.

13. Masson, "The French Navy—Today and Tomorrow," p. 11.

14. Pierre Dabezies, "The Defence of France and the Defence of Europe," in *R.U.S.I. and Brassey's Defence Yearbook 1974,* Royal United Services Institute for Defence Studies (ed.), (London: Brassey's, 1974), pp. 111–112.

15. France, *Livre Blanc,* vol. 1, pp. 22–25.

16. Ibid., pp. 24–25.

17. Ibid., p. 25: "Enfin, en temps de paix comme en temps de crise, la Marine permet au Gouvernement, par la démonstration de sa seule présence, en Méditerranée, en Atlantique, et ailleurs, dans le monde entier, d'affirmer sa volonté d'action ou de médiation."

18. Moore, *Jane's,* pp. 109–132.

19. Moore, "France and Her Navy," p. 10.

20. Masson, "The French Navy—Today and Tomorrow," pp. 11–13.

21. France, Ministre chargé de la défense nationale, 16 September 1970, quoted in Jean-Pierre Quéneudec, "La remise en cause du droit de la mer," in Societé française pour le droit internationale, *Actualités du droit de la mer* (Paris: A. Pedone, 1973), p. 27. "La mer redevient aujourd'hui une préoccupation fondamentale des États. . . Elle devient également pour les nations, le domaine à la fois de leur indépendence et de leur puissance."

22. On October 14, 1975, a French naval task force composed of the aircraft carrier *Clemenceau,* the destroyer *Bouvet,* the missile frigate *Tourville,* and two tankers was sent to the Indian Ocean to demonstrate the French concern with their sea connection to the oil-producing states. Reuter (London), 14 October 1974, in *Foreign Broadcast Information Service,* VII, 15 October 1974, p. L2.

23. On March 26, 1976, the French government protested the presence of a Soviet intelligence vessel lying off of Brest, the Atlantic port of the French SSBN fleet. *New York Times,* 27 March 1976, p. 2.

24. None of the nearly 300 entries in the Law of the Sea Institute, *Marine Policy, Law and Economics Bibliography* (Kingston, R.I.: University of Rhode Island, 1970 and 1973) relate to French ocean policy. The authoritative French ocean law bibliography lists only five references to French national maritime policy as opposed to thirty-nine for the United States and eleven for the Soviet Union. A. Bermes and J.-P. Levy, *Bibliographie du droit de la mer* (Paris: Editions techniques, 1974). Two examples of French work concerning international law of the sea questions are

Societé française pour le droit internationale, *Actualités du droit de la mer,* and René-Jean Dupuy and Alain Piquemal, "National Appropriation of Maritime Areas," in Institut du droit de la paix et du développement, *Montpelier Conference May 25-26, 1972* (Nice, France: Institut du droit de la paix et du développement, 1972). But see the following article which was published too late to aid in the preparation of text: Jean-Pierre Beurier and Patrick Cadenat "Les positions de la France à l'égard de la mer", *Révue Génerale Droit International Public* 79 (1975):1028.

25. United Nations, General Assembly, *Third United Nations Conference on the Law of the Sea* (A/CONF.62/INF.3), 1974, pp. 19–20.

26. Sanguinetti, *Le fracas des armes,* pp. 35–36.

27. France, Ambassade, Service de presse et d'information, *France* (May 1975):7.

28. "French Trade Hurt by Lack of Ships," *Christian Science Monitor,* 6 October 1975, p. 18.

29. Ibid.

30. France, *France* (November 1974):3, (August–September 1974):6–7, and (May 1973):7.

31. France, Centre National pour l'Exploitation des Océans, *Bulletin d'Information* (February 1975):19.

32. European Communities, Directorate General Press and Information, *Newsletter on the Common Agricultural Policy,* No. 8 (November 1970):7.

33. Mark W. Janis, "The Roles of Regional Law of the Sea," *San Diego Law Review* 12 (No. 3, 1975):559–561.

34. U.S., Department of the Interior, Geological Survey, *Summary Petroleum and Selected Mineral Statistics for 120 Countries, Including Offshore Areas,* Geological Survey Professional Paper No. 817 (Washington, D.C.: Government Printing Office, 1973), p. 40.

35. UN, *Law of the Sea Conference* (A/CONF.62/SR.37), p. 6.

36. Ibid. (A/CONF.62/C.2/SR.23), p. 7.

37. Ibid., pp. 7–9.

38. Ibid., p. 11.

39. Michel Debré, "France's Global Strategy," *Foreign Affairs* 49 (April 1971):402.

5

Coastal Navy States

The sea power of a coastal navy state differs from that of the naval powers in terms both of its function and its size. The coastal navy is principally intended to protect the coast, to defend the state against maritime attack, and to enforce national maritime regulations. It is rarely tasked with distant water missions. Furthermore, no coastal navy has a functioning SSBN, and thus none has a nuclear deterrence role. In terms of size, the coastal navies are significantly outgunned by the major navies. The four naval powers together have six times as many aircraft carriers, four times as many cruisers, more destroyers, and nearly as many frigates as all 122 coastal navies combined.[1]

Classifying all the rest of the world's navies as coastal navies is a useful way of distinguishing them from the four major, blue water, SSBN navies, but the resulting group of maritime forces is very diverse. After denominating the superpower navies of the United States and the Soviet Union as first-class and the fleets of Great Britain and France as second-class, coastal navies can then be broken down into three more classes.

Some 21 third-class navies have more than 10 major surface combatants (cruisers, destroyers, and frigates), usually some submarines, and occasionally an aircraft carrier.[a] These third-class navies typically have between 80 and 250 vessels in all. The Brazilian Navy, for example, has an aircraft carrier, a cruiser, 15 destroyers, 3 frigates, 8 conventional submarines, and some 65 other craft.[2]

---

[a]These breakdowns into naval classes are only rough estimations by the author. The figures are all drawn from John E. Moore (ed.), *Jane's Fighting Ships 1974–1975* (London: Macdonald & Co., 1974). Those countries with third-class navies are Argentina, Australia, Brazil, Canada, Chile, China, Germany (Federal Republic), Greece, India, Italy, Japan, Korea (South), Mexico, Netherlands, Peru, Portugal, Spain, Sweden, Taiwan, Turkey, and Venezuela.

Another 29 fourth-class navies have at least one, but no more than 10, major surface combatants.[b] Fourth-class navies have no aircraft carriers, rarely a cruiser, and number about 50 vessels in all. A not unusual fourth-class fleet, the Finnish Navy, has 2 frigates and 62 other vessels, including corvettes, gunboats, and patrol craft.[3]

Finally, the remaining 72 minor maritime forces can be termed fifth-class navies.[c] A fifth-class navy has no major surface combatants and rarely more than a dozen vessels in all. The Navy of Kenya is a typical fifth-class navy with seven patrol craft, of which the largest is 123 feet with two guns.[4] But fifth-class navies can be as small as that of Tonga, which has only a single 40-foot boat armed with a machine gun.[5]

The geographical situations of coastal navy states differ at least as much as their naval strengths. Australia, Canada, and Chile have long coasts fronting on the open oceans. Iraq, West Germany, and Zaire have narrow outlets to the sea. Denmark, Indonesia, Malaysia, Morocco, Spain, and Turkey border vital international straits. Finland, Israel, Japan, and Kuwait depend enormously on passage through the straits of others. The Bahamas, Indonesia, and the Philippines consist of many islands forming archipelagos.

These geographical variations tend to diminish the cohesiveness of coastal navy state interests which result from their common position of naval inferiority vis-à-vis the four naval powers. Political and ideological differences also split the coastal navy states. But a sense of a coastal navy state position does emerge from an analysis of the policy of coastal navy states toward the three issues concerning sea power and the law of the sea.

Passage through Straits

The difference between the straits position of the coastal navy states and that of the naval powers is clearly seen in the

---

[b]Fourth-class fleets belong to Belgium, Bulgaria, Burma, Colombia, Cuba, Denmark, Dominican Republic, Ecuador, Egypt, Finland, Germany (Democratic Republic), Indonesia, Iran, Libya, Malaysia, Morocco, New Zealand, Nigeria, Norway, Philippines, Pakistan, Poland, South Africa, Sri Lanka, Thailand, Tunisia, Uruguay, Vietnam, and Yugoslavia.

---

[c]There are too many fifth-class navies to list here. Perhaps "navy" is too strong a word to describe these maritime forces which even include the river patrol boats of land-locked countries such as Austria, Mali, and Paraguay.

proceedings of the Second Committee at the Caracas Conference. International straits were the topic of debate from the eleventh meeting on July 22, 1974, to the fifteenth meeting on July 25, 1974.[6] The naval powers supported the draft articles on straits prepared by the Soviet Union and that prepared by the United Kingdom, both of which provided for the right of transit passage for straits, as discussed above. Some coastal state support was given to draft articles prepared by Malaysia, Morocco, Oman, and Yemen, which maintained only innocent passage rights for vessels and which, in Article 15, provided that the coastal state may require prior notification for the passage of warships.[7]

In the debate at Caracas on straits, the three opening statements were made by coastal states bordering straits—Spain on Gibraltar, Iran on Hormuz, and Denmark on the Danish straits. All argued for some form of innocent passage regime, though Denmark was willing to grant free passage for straits (unlike the Danish straits) not traditionally overlapped by territorial waters.[8] Britain rose to defend its draft articles which, importantly, did not distinguish between the passage of merchant vessels and that of warships.[9] This, however, is a distinction which is crucial for many coastal navy states, which favor free transit for merchant ships but treat the passage of men of war more suspiciously. As the representative from Sri Lanka explained,

[A] distinction should be made between the passage of merchant vessels and that of warships. As a developing country with an export-import economy, desirous of increasing its share in an expanding world trade, Sri Lanka supported the view that it was in the interests of the world economy that passage of merchant vessels should be unimpeded except in circumstances such as *force majeure* or navigational hazards, and that the right to transit passage should be recognized for all ships without discrimination as to flag, point of origin or destination. . . .

On the other hand . . . Sri Lanka, which was committed to a nuclear-free zone and to zones of peace, obviously could not advocate or encourage the passage of foreign warships.[10]

Sri Lanka went on to say that it was willing to compromise and suggested special regulations for warship transit, including prior notification to the coastal state and the right of the coastal state to exclude warships that failed to obey national laws and regulations.[11]

After the Soviet delegate noted that his country's only access to the Atlantic and Pacific were through straits and that, accordingly, unilateral arrangements for straits were unacceptable,[12] East Germany, Cuba, and Mongolia all voiced their support for free passage through straits.[13] Soviet bloc countries have rallied to Soviet naval interests regardless of their own naval strengths or national geography. Cuba declared that innocent passage rules were a plot of the imperialists and would give the United States the means of obstructing maritime transit to Cuba.[14] This "plot" was, however, rather far from the legal preferences of the United States, which remarked that "the inadequacies of the traditional doctrine of innocent passage were well known."[15]

Neither the Soviet Union nor the United States had yet to respond to Sri Lanka's distinction between the passage of merchant vessels and that of warships. Tanzania reemphasized the difference:

[I]t was necessary to distinguish between ships performing national duties and ships performing international duties. Merchant ships performed an international duty and their passage through straits should not be hampered in any way . . .

With regard to warships, they were not, in his delegation's opinion, in the service of the international community: rather, they were used to further the foreign policy objectives of a few States. Warships should therefore give notification of passage and should not pass through a strait secretly because of the risks to the coastal State. In any case, why the secrecy for warships if their passage was peaceful?[16]

Canada pointed out that coastal states may seek to control straits transit to regulate the environment and prevent pollution.[17] But the chief reason why states may seek to limit the transit of warships is national security. Peru argued that the passage of warships was neither in the community interest nor an innocent use of the oceans.[18] Perhaps the harshest attack on the straits position of the naval powers was launched by China. The Chinese delegate specifically rejected the Soviet proposal for free transit of straits and contended that there must be tighter regulation of warship passage than merchant passage.[19] China accused the Soviet Union of obliterating the distinction between merchant ships and warships under a "smoke-screen of 'all ships.' "[20] Then followed the most direct attack on the naval interests of any naval power:

The Soviet representative at the preceding meeting had referred to the increase in the volume of international trade. That increase could hardly have been brought about by the free passage of warships and nuclear submarines through straits.

That super-Power was also peddling its claim for free passage of warships through straits under the label of safe-guarding collective security. But it had substantially increased its fleet in the Mediterranean and in the Indian Ocean, thus directly threatening the security of the countries in those regions, infringing their sovereignty and interfering in their internal affairs. That action could in no way be described as a measure of collective security; on the contrary it had greatly aggravated insecurity in the world.[21]

The Chinese speaker concluded by stating that free transit of straits by military vessels could not be acceptable in a law of the sea treaty since free transit was nothing more than a superpower plot to carry out an expansionist policy of world hegemony.[22]

Without joining in China's sweeping condemnation of the naval powers, Yemen and Ghana followed in demanding less preferential treatment for the passage of naval vessels.[23] The United States, however, rejected discriminatory treatment of warships as both unrealistic and dangerous for international stability.[24]

Thus, the line between the naval powers and the coastal navy states on naval transit through straits was clearly drawn at Caracas. In subsequent speeches, Oman, Spain, Algeria, Nigeria, Albania, Kuwait, and Democratic Yemen all supported innocent passage regimes at least partly on the grounds that they would give coastal states better legal justification for regulating the passage of foreign warships.[25] Bulgaria and the Ukraine from the Soviet bloc countered and promoted free transit.[26]

Very few coastal navy states rely on straits to accomplish naval missions, but most do depend on passage through straits for their international commerce. Thus, the distinction they draw between a free right of passage for merchant vessels and a circumscribed right for warships is a natural result of their own maritime interests. Without blue water capabilities and without SSBNs, the coastal navy has little reason to venture far from home and through the straits bordered by other countries. Since the principal duty of the coastal navy is local defense, this mission will be facilitated by prior notice of the passage of warships by the naval powers or by another coastal navy state.

The straits issue is the one on which the interests of the naval powers and those of coastal navy states most diverge. The position of the coastal navy states varies from the outright hostility to naval free transit, as expressed by China, to the firm support of the straits policies of the naval powers, as given by the Soviet Union's allies. The bulk of coastal navy state opinion lies in between, neither condemning the naval powers for seeking free military transit, but not quitting in their own determination to regulate, as much as possible, naval transit through straits.[27]

Transit along Coasts

The debate at Caracas did not display as much coastal navy state concern with naval transit along coasts as with naval passage through straits. Neither the discussion about the territorial sea nor that regarding the 200-mile economic zone devoted even minimal attention to problems of naval use.[28] The proceedings reflected a general consensus in favor of a 12-mile territorial sea and of the new economic zone. Insofar as there was a clash between the maritime powers and the coastal states, it dealt with economic rather than naval issues.

This relative absence of concern about naval transit along coasts dates back to the debates in the Ad Hoc and Permanent Seabed Committees. There, too, the issues had been chiefly economic. But some traces of coastal state naval interests can be reported. Peru, for example, mentioned naval transit in 1971, in a speech defending its claimed 200-mile territorial sea:

[T]he extension of his country's territorial seas to a distance of 200 miles could affect non-innocent intentions of some powers and might, of course, interfere with the long-term military and strategic plans of certain Powers. It was unable to see, however, that it would affect international trade or the right of innocent passage in any way whatsoever.[29]

A more thorough consideration of the transit of the warships of the naval powers came shortly thereafter by Oribe from Uruguay. Since it is one of the few expositions by a delegate from a coastal navy state about the relationship between territorial seas and the exercise of military power, it deserves special attention. Oribe remarked that it was important to look at the political and security effects of expanded territorial seas as well as at their economic effects.[30] Strategically, he adopted the perspective of Mahan and saw the high seas as simply an arena for the free exercise of the sea power of the major states:[31]

The main consequence of the exercise of naval power in peace-time by the large maritime Powers was that the coastal States found themselves in the position of being neighbors of the dominant naval Powers, with which their common frontier was determined by the outer limit of their territorial waters. Since the big naval Powers had never recognized a breadth of more than three miles for the territorial seas of coastal States, the common frontier had been, and still largely was, situated three miles from the shores of coastal States.[32]

Oribe, thus, saw the support of the naval powers for narrow territorial seas not as a defense of the internationality of the oceans, but as an attempt to put their sea power as close as possible to coastal states.[33]

The Uruguayan delegate's analysis of the use of the high seas by the naval powers is remarkably close to that of advocates of naval presence like Turner, Gorshkov, and the *Livre Blanc.* Not unnaturally, Oribe's attitude toward naval presence is the very opposite of that of the spokesmen of the naval powers. Blue water navies have the capability of showing force off the coasts of others. Uruguay's biggest warships are three 300-foot frigates and two 200-foot corvettes.[34] It is a fleet well suited for some coastal defense and for enforcement of national maritime regulations. But, clearly, Uruguay is unable to make much of a naval presence off any nation's shores and might well be more interested in a rule that kept all navies far from foreign coasts.

Other states have mentioned national security interests as one motivation for seeking greater territorial limits. China, for example, has accused the superpowers of ignoring the reasonable defense needs of coastal states.[35] But, generally, naval concerns have taken a back seat to economic interests for almost all coastal states with regard to the extension of coastal jurisdiction. Most seem willing to trade transit rights for the right of the coastal state to control economic exploitation in the 200-mile zone.

Coastal states have been less eager to grant freedom of research within the economic zone. In a statement typical of many coastal navy states, the delegate from the Congo at Caracas called for coastal state regulation of all maritime research within the 200-mile zone and then, beyond that limit, control of research by international machinery.[36] Both of these sorts of control would be directly opposed to the research interests of the naval powers. Austria, Belgium, Bolivia, and fourteen other states presented "Draft Articles on Marine Scientific Research" at Caracas.[37] Article 5 provided that research within territorial waters could be conducted only with the consent of the coastal state.[38] Article 6 allowed scientific research in the economic zone but only with prior notification to the coastal state, which was also entitled to all the fruits of the investigation.[39] Beyond the economic zone, Article 7 preserved the freedom of research.[40] These articles, although probably aimed principally at economically related research, could have an important impact on military research, putting large areas of the oceans under coastal state control.

Other attempts to limit the operations of the naval powers off foreign coasts have been made outside the context of the law of the sea negotiations. The most well known is the effort by India and others to restrict the activities of major navies in the Indian Ocean. In 1971, the General Assembly passed Resolution 2832 (XXVI) which designated the Indian Ocean a "zone of peace" and called upon the great powers to withdraw their military presence from the area, seeking to ensure that:

Warships and military aircraft may not use the Indian Ocean for any threat or use of force against the sovereignty, territorial integrity or independence of any littoral or hinterland State of the Indian Ocean in contravention of the purposes and principles of the Charter of the United Nations.[41]

But, at the Law of the Sea Conference, the coastal navy states are more interested in securing the economic resources of the 200-mile zone than in pushing the naval operations of the maritime powers that far from their shores. This is a result not only of the high priority given to economic development by most states, but also of the sentiment that most of the naval activities of the maritime powers are directed toward each other and do not directly challenge the sovereignty of coastal countries. Once the economic issues of the oceans are better settled, however, it is likely that the national security interests of the coastal navy states will reemerge. In the future, there will be more expressions like those of Oribe of Uruguay and greater efforts to restrict the coastal transit of the naval powers.

Military Use of the Seabed

The speech that began the current round of United Nations law of the sea negotiations gave considerable attention to the dangers of an arms race on the ocean floor. Ambassador Pardo addressed the First Committee of the General Assembly for a morning and part of the afternoon on November 1, 1967.[42] After discussing the wealth of seabed resources, Pardo turned to "grave considerations of a security and defence nature that impel the major Powers to appropriate areas of the ocean floor for their own exclusive use."[43] He cited the installation of seabed devices to track SSBNs, of antiballistic missile systems, of offensive nuclear missiles, and of other fixed military weapons, as dangers that the international community must try to avoid.[44] Otherwise, he said:

[W]e could expect an immediate and rapid escalation of the arms race in the seas, if any of the hypothetical developments that I have mentioned were known to have taken place beyond the limits of the geophysical continental shelf. There would certainly be a race to occupy accessible strategic areas on the ocean floor without much regard to the claims of other states.[45]

Accordingly, Pardo urged that it be agreed that the seabed be devoted to exclusively peaceful purposes.[46]

Despite this initiative, the real concern with the military use of the seabed has been displayed not by coastal navy states, but by the two superpowers. The Soviet Union led the early fight for complete demilitarization of the seabed in the Seabed Committees and in the Eighteen-Nation Disarmament Conference. But in 1969 the Soviet Union chose to accept the United States proposal to ban only weapons of mass destruction actually fixed on the ocean floor. This Soviet switch shocked the other members of the Disarmament Conference, most of whom had rallied to the early Soviet stand.[47] With few amendments, the superpowers were able to pass their joint measure through the Conference and through the General Assembly, from which it emerged as the 1971 Seabed Arms Control Treaty.[48]

Occasionally a coastal navy state will argue that there should be complete seabed demilitarization à la Pardo. Libya, for one, proposed in 1969 that there be:

(a) prohibition of the establishment of military installations and the placing of weapons of mass destruction in the area [the deep seabed];
(b) prohibition of the establishment of any object containing nuclear weapons and the stationing of such weapons on the sea-bed or its sub-soil; and
(c) prohibition of the establishment of military bases, installations or fortifications, and of the testing of any type of weapon on the sea-bed.[49]

But, generally, coastal state concern about the seabed has been more economic than military. There seems, again, an attitude that these military operations are more a part of the United States/

Soviet naval confrontation than a threat to third states. The coastal states have been, though, more sensitive about military installations on their continental shelves, and Latin American countries, especially have made a special point of resisting any such use of the offshore plateau.[50]

There need be little real interest by coastal navies in the usual sort of deep-sea military uses. No coastal navy state has the technological capacity to maintain ocean floor listening devices, the principal current military use of the seabed. And insofar as the superpowers maintain such devices, they are aimed at submarine detection and the balance of nuclear terror, not at coastal navies. Of the three issues of naval concern, the military use of the seabed is the one of least interest to coastal navy states.

Notes

1. John E. Moore (ed.), *Jane's Fighting Ships 1974–1975* (London: Macdonald & Co., 1974), pp. 642–643.

2. Ibid., p. 43.

3. Ibid., p. 105.

4. Ibid., p. 214.

5. Ibid., p. 320.

6. United Nations, *Third United Nations Conference on the Law of the Sea, Official Records Volume II,* 1975, pp. 123–142.

7. Ibid., *Volume III,* pp. 192–195.

8. Ibid., *Volume II,* pp. 123–124.

9. Ibid., p. 125.

10. Ibid., p. 126.

11. Ibid.

12. Ibid., p. 127.

13. Ibid., pp. 127–128.

14. Ibid., p. 127.

15. Ibid., p. 128.

16. Ibid., p. 129.

17. Ibid., p. 130.

18. Ibid., pp. 131–132.

19. Ibid., p. 133.

20. Ibid.

21. Ibid., pp. 133–134.

22. Ibid., p. 134.

23. Ibid., pp. 134–135.

24. Ibid., p. 135.

25. Ibid., pp. 135–142.

26. Ibid., pp. 139–141.

27. For a description of the straits debate from an author of a coastal navy state (Iran), see D. Momtaz, "La Question des détroits à la troisième conférence des Nations-Unies sur le droit de la mer," *Annuaire Français de Droit International* 20 (1974):841.

28. United Nations, *Conference Volume II,* pp. 98–121 and 170–226.

29. United Nations, General Assembly, *Permanent Sea-Bed Committee Summary Records* (A/AC.138/SC.II/SR.6), 1971, p. 27.

30. Ibid. (A/AC.138/SC.II/SR.16), 1971, p. 176.

31. Ibid., pp. 176–177.

32. Ibid., p. 177.

33. Ibid.

34. Moore (ed.), *Jane's,* pp. 585–586.

35. United Nations, *Permanent Sea-Bed Committee* (A/AC.138/ SC.II/SR.55), 1973, pp. 81–82.

36. UN, *Conference on the Law of the Sea, Official Records Volume II,* p. 353.

37. Ibid., *Volume III,* pp. 266–267.

38. Ibid., p. 267.

39. Ibid.

40. Ibid.

41. United Nations, General Assembly, *Resolution 2832 (XXVI),* 16 December 1971.

42. United Nations, General Assembly, Twenty-second Session, *First Committee 1515th Meeting* (A/C.1/PV.1515), 1 November 1967, pp. 1–15, and *First Committee 1516th Meeting* (A/C.1/ PV.1516), 1 November 1967, pp. 1–3.

43. Ibid., *1515th Meeting,* p. 6.

44. Ibid., p. 7.

45. Ibid.

46. Ibid.

47. Evan Luard, *The Control of the Sea-Bed* (London: Heinemann, 1974), pp. 97–106.

48. Ibid., pp. 106–108.

49. UN, *Permanent Sea-Bed Committee* (A/AC.138/SC.1/SR.8), 1969, p. 82.

50. Luard, *The Control of the Sea-Bed,* pp. 101–102.

6

Navies and the Development of the Law of the Sea

Before going further, it will be useful at this point to return to the discussion of the relationship between navies and the law of the sea considered in the Introduction. Viewing this relationship from the perspective of Professor McDougal gives us a good idea of where we have been and where we are going. In *Public Order of the Oceans* McDougal and Burke distinguish "three different processes: the process of *interaction* by which the oceans are enjoyed, the process of *claim* by which interests are asserted, and the process of *authoritative decision* by which interests are honored and protected."[1] A navy figures in all three processes.

The preceding five chapters considered navies in the first two processes. The examination of naval missions was directed to the process of interaction. The navy may well be one of the principal national maritime actors enjoying ocean use. The study of naval roles and reflections in national ocean policies looked to the process of claim. Naval interests are an important component in the formulation and expression of national claims to ocean law.

This chapter turns to the third process, authoritative decision. The international authoritative decision process generates law of the sea both by custom and by convention. Customary law of the sea is the result of consistent and accepted maritime practice. Conventionary law of the sea is the result of negotiations yielding written rules. Naval operations may contribute to the growth of customary international law whereas naval interests may be crucial to the emergence of the law of the sea by convention.

States may use their navies to demonstrate and enforce their perceptions of the proper law of the sea. If such naval operations are consistent, effective, and accepted, customary law of the sea may develop. But if such naval operations are inconsistent, ineffective, or resisted, chaos may result.

Naval interests may be reconciled in law of the sea negotiations and be protected and compromised in meaningful law of the sea conventions. But naval interests may also lead to discord and a breakdown in diplomatic efforts. Since the international authoritative decision process is decentralized among sovereign states, disagreement will frustrate the development of the law of the sea.

Both the customary and conventionary aspects of the development of the law of the sea are treated in this chapter. The first part considers the role of navies in the development of the customary law of the sea. The second part looks at the role of naval interests in the law of the sea negotiations at the Third Law of the Sea Conference. In both parts, special attention is paid to the potential of navies to contribute and to impede the development of the law of the sea.

Sea Power and the Development of Customary Law of the Sea

The traditional law of the sea was much more the creature of customary than conventionary development. The practice of the chief maritime nations was the basis for most of the rules of ocean order in the 19th and early 20th centuries.[2] Not until 1958 were general conventions drafted that pretended to cover the main body of the law of the sea, and these four Geneva Conventions were more a codification of existing customary law than they were an establishment of new legal rules.

In the development of the law of the sea by custom, individual states make claims about the nature of the law by way of their own maritime practice. If these claims are left unchallenged and if the practice forms a pattern and is long-standing, then a new customary law may be said to develop. If, on the other hand, claims by one state are challenged by counterclaims from other states, and if one nation's practice is countered by the contrary or opposing practice of another nation, then the customary process continues until either the claim or the counterclaim predominates. This customary process of developing international law need not be neat or easy. It may never lead to results. But, where nations cannot or will not agree on written rules, the customary process is an alternative way to develop international law. The old ocean order, based on customary development, is perhaps the best example of how effective a customary process may be.

In the customary process, naval operations and the exercise of sea power may play a vital role because naval activities are an authoritative and forceful expression of state interest and policy. Naval operations can be part of this customary process in several forms. Ships and planes can enforce claims to increased national maritime jurisdiction by attempting to force other vessels from other states to leave the claimed areas or to pay fees or obey national laws. Or navies can be used to assert the freedoms of the high seas and to resist national claims. Navies can be used to assert national claims over straits and counterclaims to free or innocent passage. Navies may protect national or international deep-sea mining ventures or may interfere with them. Navies can protect the passage of merchant vessels, or they can interrupt them.

But there are great possibilities of dangerous conflict when navies are used in the customary development of the law of the sea. Navies are an instrument of force, and they will be construed as such. The use of sea power may further unsettle troublesome situations. Naval activities may be counterproductive and only aggravate differences among states.

A good example of the potential for naval operations to aggravate a maritime dispute was the 1972–1973 Anglo-Icelandic Cod War. On September 1, 1972, the Icelandic government unilaterally proclaimed a 50-mile exclusive fishing zone. This claim was protested by the United Kingdom because British trawlermen were the principal foreign fishers in the new zone. Great Britain argued, *inter alia,* that Iceland was bound by a 1961 agreement either to secure the advance consent of Britain or to win a judgment from the International Court of Justice before extending her fishing waters beyond a 12-mile zone. This agreement was the concession won by Great Britain in the negotiations which settled an earlier Cod War in 1958 when Iceland extended her limits to 12 miles. The United Kingdom rejected the new Icelandic claim, explaining that Iceland had neither gained Britain's consent nor secured a favorable court ruling. Iceland, in turn, rejected the British argument and noted that the depletion of fish stocks in the zone and Iceland's exceptional dependence on fishing meant that the 1961 agreement was no longer binding and, furthermore, that Iceland's claim was justified by the new developments in the law of the sea in claiming an extended fishing zone. For thirteen months in 1972 to 1973, British fishing trawlers and Icelandic patrol boats clashed in the disputed zone.[3]

In the spring of 1973, the Icelandic patrol boats (the only naval force which Iceland had) stepped up their interference with British fishing. The British trawlermen withdrew from the 50-mile zone and refused to return unless accompanied by the Royal Navy, which to this point had not intervened.[4] Great Britain had a choice. If the Navy was not sent in and if the fishermen did not return, then Iceland would have effectively won the Cod War and begun to establish an invaluable legal precedent since the United Kingdom would no longer be exercising its historical fishing rights nor be meaningfully making a counterclaim to Iceland's 50-mile claim. If the Royal Navy was sent in, the trawlermen would return, and Britain would continue to assert its claim to high seas fishing rights in the disputed zone. On May 20, 1973, the Royal Navy in the form of three frigates escorted some fifteen British trawlers back into the zone.[5]

But the introduction of the Royal Navy was really the beginning of the end for Great Britain. The arrival of British warships greatly upset the Icelandic population and gave the left-wing Icelandic government the additional public support it needed to threaten to throw the United States out of its NATO air base at Keflavik. The Keflavik base is considered an essential post for NATO to monitor the passage of Russian submarines in the North Atlantic.[6] When the Royal Navy moved into the 50-mile zone, the Icelandic government complained of an invasion and that the navy of a NATO country was attacking Iceland instead of protecting it.[7] On June 3, 1973, the Prime Minister of Iceland told the United States that unless the Royal Navy quit the zone, Iceland would demand a revision of the treaty giving the United States the right to maintain the Keflavik base.[8]

Since it appeared that the entry of British naval forces into the Cod War was providing the Icelandic government with the cause and popular support to endanger the Keflavik base, the United States and NATO entered the dispute. Kissinger-like, the Secretary-General of NATO, Luns of the Netherlands, went from Iceland to Britain and back again to try to find a settlement for this fishing dispute which now threatened NATO security.[9] The Keflavik base was a higher priority for the United States and NATO than were British fishing rights. Despite the fact that the United States had protested Latin American fishing claims for almost three decades, the United States did not come to the support of the United Kingdom. Neither did the United States openly support Iceland, but it was clear that the United States preferred a settlement and would accept a 50-mile Icelandic fishing zone as a necessary precondition. As a result of Luns's mediation, the United Kingdom agreed to withdraw the Royal Navy on October 2, 1973.[10] On October 16, 1973, the United Kingdom and Iceland agreed to sign an interim 2-year agreement, which was formally concluded on November 13, 1973. The agreement reduced the number of British trawlers which could fish in the zone, restricted the British catch and the area in which Britain could fish, and gave the Icelandic coast guard the right to patrol the waters.[11] Iceland had won the Cod War.

By sending in naval forces the British government had only stiffened Icelandic resolve to win the Cod War. It had precipitated the threats to the Keflavik base and brought the United States and NATO into the dispute predisposed to favor the Icelandic cause. Faced with the threat of its trawlermen to withdraw from the 50-mile zone, Britain might have tried responding with promises of financial aid similar to those used by the United States to keep its tuna fishermen operating in Latin American waters.[12] By using the Royal Navy, Great Britain increased tension, thereby yielding a result opposite to that desired. Now that Iceland has claimed a 200-mile fishing zone and a new Anglo-Icelandic Cod War has begun, it is exceedingly doubtful that the use of the Royal Navy will lead to any more satisfactory conclusion for Britain that it did before.[13]

More successful have been the naval operations asserting rights to navigation. Beginning with the Royal Navy's disputed passage through the Corfu Channel in 1946,[14] the British and United States navies have been particularly active in demonstrating rights to unimpeded navigation. The Royal Navy and the United States Navy have made shows of force to assert transit rights through the Red Sea and the Straits of Tiran to Israel.[15] The United States Navy has sent warships through the Indonesian straits to demonstrate the right of passage in the face of Indonesian claims.[16]

Most controversial among the naval operations protecting rights to ocean transit was the *Mayaguez* incident. After a Cambodian gunboat seized the United States merchant ship *Mayaguez* on May 12, 1975, the United States used aircraft, Marines, and naval vessels to retake the ship.[17] Although the prompt United States action was due in large part to the desire to demonstrate that the United States had not lost the will to fight after the Vietnam defeat, the *Mayaguez* incident was also a reaffirmation of the United States intent to protect the rights of passage on international waters.[18]

If the United Nations law of the sea negotiations fail to reach conventions that are generally accepted by the world community, it is very likely that there will be many more disputes about maritime matters which lead to conflict. In such a situation, the role of sea power in developing the law of the sea by custom will be especially crucial. The fate of the Royal Navy in the Cod War should be good proof that naval superiority will not necessarily yield victory in conflicts over the resolution of international law questions. Naval force can be used only within an international political context, and it may be that naval operations will awaken more opposition that they will quiet. But if naval operations assert legal rights which are more generally accepted in the international community than not, then consistent naval practice has a good chance of success. One key distinction between the Cod War and the naval operations promoting navigation rights is simply the distinction between Britain's claim to be able to fish up to 12 miles from Iceland (a claim not accepted by many states) and the British and United States claims to free navigation rights (claims accepted by most states). Naval force of the naval powers is bound to be viewed suspiciously by other countries. It will be most acceptable if used in causes shared with other countries. Certainly one of the factors in the United States decision not to use naval force to protect United States tuna fishermen off Latin America must have been that United States naval activities against the country's southern neighbors would awaken a great amount of resentment and hostility.

Naval Interests and the Law of the Sea Negotiations

The hazards of developing the law of the sea by claim and counterclaim make it all the more desirable that the new ocean order be framed by international conventions. As set out in the Introduction, United Nations law of the sea negotiations have been proceeding in the Seabed Committee since 1968 and at the Third Law of the Sea Conference in Caracas in 1974, Geneva in 1975, and New York in 1976.[19] Although the four naval powers might have a predominance of naval forces, they certainly have far from a predominance of the votes in the conference setting. Developing countries marshal not only a majority of the votes, but a working two-thirds of all attending states. Still, it is broadly understood that law of the sea conventions that do not have the support of the maritime powers and especially the support of the United States and the Soviet Union have little chance of effective implementation. Similarly, the naval powers need the votes of the developing countries to produce a treaty at all. Since the naval powers have many other ocean uses such as fishing, shipping, mineral exploitation, and research to protect, there is a real need for give-and-take on all sides.

Although this text has sometimes spoken of a nation's ocean policy as a finished product, in fact the policy may remain quite flexible even when a national delegation reaches a negotiating session. This flexibility may be only a result of an inability of the national decision-making process to reconcile various ocean interests, but it is also a vital asset if various national policies are to be compromised in order to reach international agreement. National ocean policies too well settled might lead to stalemate.

Naval participation in the national ocean policy process does not end in the nation's capital. Naval representatives accompany the national negotiating teams to the law of the sea meetings and maintain a naval input while national ocean policies are being compromised. Not only the naval powers but African, Asian, Latin American, and every other sort of state has sent navy or defense delegates to the Law of the Sea Conference.[20] Joined by other special-interest representatives for fishing, minerals, and research, these naval representatives advise on technical questions, channel information about the negotiations back home to their respective establishments, and serve as checks to ensure that their perceived interests are not too greatly compromised in the negotiations. Thus, naval interests are forwarded not only by the settled national ocean policies of states but by naval representatives on the spot.

The impact of naval interests on the law of the sea negotiations can be clearly seen in the *Informal Single Negotiating Text* which issued from the 1975 Geneva Conference and the *Revised Single Negotiating Text* issuing from the 1976 New York Conference.[21] These texts have four parts: one presented by the chairmen of each of the three major committees of the conference and one presented by the president of the conference dealing with the settlement of disputes. The *Informal Single Negotiating Text* was intended only to be an aid to the ongoing law of the sea negotiations. It has no legal force. It also served as the basis for the *Revised Single Negotiating Text,* which reflects the months of negotiations after the Geneva session. These texts are the most concrete and comprehensive results so far from the current rounds of the law of the sea negotiations.

The parts of the texts dealing with straits, the coastal zone, and the peaceful use of the seabed were not greatly modified from the *Informal Single Negotiating Text* to the *Revised Single Negotiating Text.* This analysis considers the *Revised Single Negotiating Text* and notes the impact of naval interests on it. The text deals with many topics (deep-sea mining, fishing, pollution, and others) that are only peripherally linked to naval concerns and that display no particular impression of naval interests. Some parts, though, especially those relating to passage through straits, show that naval interests have been crucial in their formulation.

The crucial navy-related articles concerning straits in the *Revised Single Negotiating Text* are Articles 36 and 37 of Part II:

Article 36

Scope of this section

This section applies to straits which are used for international navigation between one area of the high seas or an exclusive economic zone and another area of the high seas or an exclusive economic zone.

Article 37

Right of transit passage

1. In straits referred to in article 36, all ships and aircraft enjoy the right of transit passage, which shall not be impeded, except that if the strait is formed by an island of a State bordering the strait and its mainland, transit passage shall not apply if a high seas route or a route in an exclusive economic zone of similar convenience with respect to navigational and hydrographical characteristics exists seaward of the island.

2. Transit passage is the exercise in accordance with this Chapter of the freedom of navigation and overflight solely for the purpose of continuous and expeditious transit of the strait between one area of the high seas or an exclusive economic zone and another area of the high seas or an exclusive economic zone. However, the requirement of continuous and expeditious transit does not preclude passage through the strait for the purpose of entering, leaving or returning from a State bordering the strait, subject to the conditions of entry to that State.

3. Any activity which is not an exercise of the right of transit passage through a strait remains subject to the other applicable provisions of the present Convention.[22]

Article 38 provides some duties for ships and aircraft in transit passage, but these are much less severe than those imposed for innocent passage under Articles 16 to 21. First, there is no innocent passage for aircraft. Second, submarines are, as usual in rules of innocent passage, required to surface and show their flag.[23] Third, innocent passage prohibits a long list of military activities including intelligence gathering, launching of aircraft or military devices, and weapons practice.[24] Article 38, on the other hand, includes only a more general injunction to:

(a) Proceed without delay through or over the strait;
(b) Refrain from any threat or use of force against the sovereignty, territorial integrity or political independence of States bordering straits, or in any other manner in violation of the principles of international law embodied in the Charter of the United Nations;
(c) Refrain from any activities other than those incident to their normal modes of continuous and expeditious transit unless rendered necessary by *force majeure* or by distress.[25]

The other provisions relating to transit passage provide for compliance with international regulations for safety and for pollution,[26] and with national regulations for traffic separation, oil pollution, and customs, fiscal, immigration, and sanitary control.[27] Importantly, Article 42 provides:

States bordering straits shall not hamper transit passage and shall give appropriate publicity to any danger to navigation or overflight within or over the strait of which it has knowledge. There shall be no suspension of transit passage.[28]

Innocent passage, however, may be suspended by the coastal state.[29]

It is very probable that without the influence of the four naval powers, no such provisions for transit passage would exist in the *Revised Single Negotiating Text*. Not only have straits states and others opposed the adoption of any but innocent passage rules, but there have been no significant threats to international shipping, the primary other interest which might be benefited by transit passage. The important distinctions between innocent passage and transit passage are those of concern to navies: submarine passage, overflight, military activities while in transit, and no coastal state right to suspend.

Before leaving transit passage through straits, it should be pointed out that the proposed articles would not change the status of either the Turkish or Danish straits. Article 34(c) provides that "[t]he legal regime in straits in which passage is regulated in whole or in part by long-standing international conventions in force specifically relating to such straits" shall not be affected by the new rules established in the text.[30] Thus, these two European bottlenecks for Soviet naval operations would remain governed by their restrictive treaties, while straits such as Gibraltar and Malacca vital for the United States Navy would be newly protected by the transit passage provisions.

Naval interests have been less important in influencing other segments of the *Revised Single Negotiating Text.* Territorial sea limits are restricted by Article 2 of Part II to 12 miles,[31] but pressure for 12-mile limits was widespread and did not come only from the naval powers. Beyond 12 miles it is not absolutely clear that full high seas passage rights remain. Articles 44 and 45 establish a 200-mile exclusive economic zone.[32] The naval powers fought to include this zone within the high seas and reserve certain rights for the coastal state for economic exploitation. Instead the *Revised Single Negotiating Text* creates a zone which is neither high seas nor territorial seas.[33] This was the point most at issue in the Second Committee at the New York session, but the Committee Chairman held firm, retaining the distinction from the *Informal Single Negotiating Text.*[34] The text first sets out the coastal state's economic rights in Article 44 and then in Article 46 gives other states the "freedoms of navigation and overflight."[35] This, of course, is preferable to innocent passage rights in territorial seas, but not as good as retention of freedoms of the high seas would be for navies. Rights to research in the exclusive economic zone are given to the coastal state from whom other states must get permission.[36]

The exclusive economic zone articles do not contain restrictions on other military activities. Thus, in law, there should be no problem for passing naval vessels. But with regard to shows of force, the exercise of the naval presence mission, or in using one nation's economic zone for operations against another nation, the argument might be made that these naval activities interfere with coastal state economic rights or do not fall within general rights of "navigation." Certainly, the naval powers would probably prefer a much broader grant of freedom between 12 and 200 miles. The very nature of the exclusive economic zone articles as they stand tends to establish coastal state control. The trend, therefore, from a distant-water naval perspective is bad.

Viewed as a trade-off, however, the provisions for the exclusive economic zone are not unsatisfactory for the naval powers. There is not only a distinction between the economic zone and the high seas but one between the economic zone and the territorial sea. Navigation rights are explicitly protected. The favorable articles concerning transit passage are, in part, an exchange for the grants to the coastal state in the 200-mile exclusive economic zone. This is not a bad compromise position.

With regard to the third area of naval concern, the deep seabed, Part I of the *Revised Single Negotiating Text* states in Article 8 that the area shall be used "exclusively for peaceful purposes."[37] This would seem to be nearer the avowed preference of the Soviet Union than that of the United States. But the military use of the seabed is no longer an important issue in the seabed debate. Even if the term "peaceful" is accepted, it is likely that any ocean floor listening device would be successfully tagged a means toward peace.

Another indication of naval influence in the law of the sea talks is to be found in Part IV, that part dealing with the settlement of disputes. Part IV establishes, *inter alia,* a Law of the Sea Tribunal for dispute settlement. Article 18(2)(b) provides that a ratifying party may declare that it will not be bound to submit to the Tribunal "disputes concerning military activities."[38] This military-activities exception reflects the usual demand of states not to submit their armed forces to any form of outside control, but, for the naval powers at least, it might be counterproductive. Coastal states may use the exception either if they choose it or if it is adopted by a naval power and refuse to submit disputes concerning that naval power's activities when the coastal state has interfered with them.[39]

Notes

1. Myres S. McDougal and William T. Burke, *The Public Order of the Oceans* (New Haven: Yale University Press, 1962), pp. 12–13.

2. C. John Colombos, *The International Law of the Sea*, 4th rev. ed. (London: Longmans, 1961), pp. 7–42.

3. For good reviews of the facts and law of the Cod War into the early months of 1973, see Stephen R. Katz, "Issues Arising in the Icelandic Fisheries Case," *International and Comparative Law Quarterly* 22 (January 1973):83–108; E. D. Brown, "Iceland's Fishery Limits: The Legal Aspects," *The World Today* 29 (February 1973):68–79; and especially Richard B. Bilder, "The Anglo-Icelandic Fisheries Dispute," *Wisconsin Law Review* (No. 1, 1973):37–132.

4. "War in the northern seas," *The Economist,* 19 May 1973, p. 104.

5. "Iceland Accuses the British of 'Invasion,' " *New York Times,* 22 May 1973, p. 3.

6. "British-Icelandic Fishing Dispute Involves Far More Than Just Cod," *New York Times,* 11 March 1976, p. 2.

7. "Iceland Recalls Envoy in Cod War," *Washington Post,* 22 May 1973, p. A4.

8. "Threat by Iceland to quit Nato in six weeks," *The Times* (London), 4 June 1973, p. 1.

9. "Nato mediation may revive cod war talks," *The Times* (London), 6 June 1973, p. 6; "Iceland to boycott Nato meeting over cod war," *The Times* (London), 7 June 1973, p. 8; "Government willing for Dr. Luns to be intermediary in dispute with Iceland," *The Times* (London), 14 June 1973, p. 8; and "New hope for renewal of cod war talks," *The Times* (London), 15 June 1973, p. 1.

10. "Britain Agrees to Pull Frigates from Icelandic Area," *New York Times,* 3 October 1973, p. 3.

11. "Iceland Reaches Accord in London," *New York Times,* 17 October 1973, p. 12; and "Iceland-United Kingdom: Agreement Concerning Fishing Rights," *International Legal Materials* 12 (November 1973):1315–1318.

12. David C. Loring, "The Fisheries Dispute," in *U.S. Foreign Policy and Peru* (Austin: University of Texas, 1972), p. 83.

13. "Cod war with Iceland: a challenge to diplomacy," *The Guardian Weekly* (London), 21 December 1975, p. 4; and "Fish Furor," *Wall Street Journal,* 25 February 1976, p. 1.

14. J. R. Hill, "The Rule of Law at Sea" (Unpublished Defence Fellow thesis, University of London, King's College, 1972), pp. 181–197.

15. Robert E. Osgood, "U.S. Security Interests in Ocean Law," *Ocean Development and International Law* 2 (Spring 1974):29.

16. Ibid.

17. Eleanor C. McDowell, "Contemporary Practice of the United States Relating to International Law," *American Journal of International Law* 69 (October 1975):875–879.

18. Ibid., p. 877.

19. See John R. Stevenson and Bernard H. Oxman, "The Preparations for the Law of the Sea Conference," *American Journal of International Law* 68 (January 1974):1; Stevenson and Oxman, "The Third United Nations Conference on the Law of the Sea: The 1974 Caracas Session," *American Journal of International Law* 69 (January 1975):1; and Stevenson and Oxman, "The Third United Nations Conference on the Law of the Sea: The 1975 Geneva Session," *American Journal of International Law* 69 (October 1975):763.

20. For example, Kenya, Nigeria, Senegal, Chile, Uruguay, Indonesia, the Philippines, Thailand, Israel, Saudi Arabia, Cuba, East Germany, Poland, Greece, Spain, and Sweden. United Nations, General Assembly, *Delegations to the Third United Nations Conference on the Law of the Sea* (A/CONF.62/INF.3), 1974, pp. 32, 41, 48, 11, 63, 27, 44, 52, 29, 47, 14, 21, 45, 23, 50, 51.

21. United Nations, General Assembly, *Third United Nations Conference on the Law of the Sea: Informal Single Negotiating Text* (A/CONF.62/WP.8/Parts I, II, III & A/CONF.62/WP.9), 1975; *Third United Nations Conference on the Law of the Sea: Revised Single Negotiating Text* (A/CONF.62/WP.8/Rev.1/Parts I, II, III & A/CONF.62/WP.9/Rev.1), 1976.

22. *Revised Single Negotiating Text,* Part II, pp. 22–23.

23. Ibid., p. 16.

24. Ibid.

25. Ibid., p. 23.

26. Ibid., p. 23.

27. Ibid., pp. 24–25.

28. Ibid., p. 25.

29. Ibid., p. 18.

30. Ibid., p. 22.

31. Ibid., p. 11.

32. Ibid., p. 26.

33. Ibid., p. 4.

34. Ibid., p. 3.

35. Ibid., pp. 26–27.

36. Ibid., p. 28.

37. Ibid., Part I, p. 13.

38. Ibid., WP.9, Part IV, p. 17.

39. Mark W. Janis, "Dispute Settlement in the Law of the Sea Convention: The Military Activities Exception," *Ocean Development and International Law,* forthcoming.

7

Navies and the New Ocean Order

Naval Interests and National Ocean Policies

The analyses in the first four chapters demonstrated the ways in which the geographic situations, the sea power, and the naval missions of the four naval powers differ. The three Western powers share excellent access to the open oceans whereas the Soviet Union is considerably more shut in by its interior position. Increasingly, the Soviet Navy is capable of and is assuming distant water naval roles, while one Western navy, the Royal Navy, is increasingly abandoning its blue water capability and intent. The Western powers depend much more on ocean communications and transportation since these link the United States with its allies in Europe and Asia. Yet, despite these differences, the law of the sea preferences of all four navies seem similar. All, more or less uniformally, stress the need to preserve high seas freedoms. To an important degree, this naval stress has been successful in legal development, both in customary practice and in the law of the sea negotiations. Most importantly, the right of transit through international straits has been protected.

But the forces, national and international, pushing to allot the seas to coastal jurisdiction are strong. Not only are there more unilateral claims to ocean space, but the direction of the law of the sea talks has been toward the recognition of increased national control. The 12-mile territorial sea and the 200-mile exclusive economic zone are probably the two best-established new proposals emanating from the Third Law of the Sea Conference. The reasons for this trend lie not so much in an anti-navy mood, but in the realization that ocean resources need to be authoritatively allocated. There are simply not enough fish to go around, nor enough oil, nor gas. And there is a need for effective ocean management if problems such as pollution and ocean safety are to be mastered.

The old ocean order based on freedoms was premised on the notion that the oceans had enough for everyone. This premise is no longer supportable. The real choice is not between the freedoms of the high seas and coastal state control; it is between international and regional management on one side and national management on the other. The 12-mile territorial sea and the 200-mile exclusive economic zone are examples of assertion of national management. The proposed international seabed authority and the regional attempts at fishery and pollution control are examples of international and regional management. All these assertions threaten to restrict naval use.

The important question is how well navies will be able to live with these new national, regional, and international regimes, and vice versa. The answer for the Soviet Navy is much less hopeful than that for the Western navies. The Soviet Union has invested vast resources in an ocean-going navy just at the time when the oceans are being carved up and regulated and when the Soviet Union, more than any other naval power, will find itself restrained by new zones of authority. One can expect that the Soviet Navy will continue to oppose new extensions of control, and because of the nature of the other Soviet ocean interests the Soviet Navy will be successful in persuading the national ocean policy process to join in its opposition.

The answers for the Western navies are much less simple. The Royal Navy, more than the others, is directed to a regional defensive role, one increasingly similar to that of the coastal navy states examined in Chapter 5. It can be suspected that, in time, the United Kingdom will consider taking advantage of its primary opponent's natural barriers and promote restraints on naval transit. Britain would probably not do so, of course, if such threatened the shipping trade or if she were opposed by her chief ally. But, on the basis of the country's naval forces and mission structure, such a restrictive policy has much to commend it.

The French Navy has greater presumptions than the British but just about as much clout. As long as the presumptions remain, naval mobility will be highly prized. But, if the naval balance in the areas bordering France should change, especially in the Mediterranean, and United States naval force is replaced by a Soviet presence, then a reexamination might well be in order. Presumably, the coastal situation of France will ultimately be of greater import than distant water possibilities.

The most difficult case of all is the United States. Certainly the strength and mobility of the United States Navy are so great that mere geographical advantage over the Soviet Navy is not enough to dictate a reevaluation of United States naval policy toward law of the sea issues. More than Britain and France, the United States has good naval reasons for promoting high seas freedoms. Perhaps the only caveat for United States naval policy would be that restrictions on high seas freedoms are inevitable and not always bad. Insofar as the United States Navy defines one of its primary functions as the containment of the Soviet Navy, it might be well to bear in mind that the Soviet Navy will usually be far worse off when freedoms are limited.

Navies and International Legal Development

Chapter 6 showed the various ways in which navies influence the development of the new ocean order. As a forceful application of state power, navies are an important factor in the emergence of the customary law of the sea. But as the Cod War study illustrated, naval power cannot alone ensure the emergence of customary law. If other states do not acquiesce in the assertion of naval power, and if other considerations prevent the continued and consistent use of naval force, the application of sea power may be only counterproductive. Certainly, if the United Nations negotiations fail to reach a consensus, naval operations will be used more frequently in attempts to settle law of the sea questions. But these operations have the potential to aggravate as well as solve ocean disputes. They will be most successful when used for causes generally accepted in the international community. When used for narrow interests, although perhaps temporarily successful, naval operations will not muster the support necessary for the establishment of customary rules of international law.

If the law of the sea negotiations do not succeed, it is very unlikely that naval interests will be blamed for the failure. The *Revised Single Negotiating Text* appears to contain a realistic group of compromises concerning naval interests in law of the sea issues. The provisions on transit passage through straits, the most important issue for the great navies, are well to the side of the naval powers. The articles of the exclusive economic zone are more finely balanced, giving the distant water navies the right of transit but not the right of research and reserving the question of how much this new navigation right in the economic zone is like a high seas right of navigation. The part on the seabed should pose no problems for ocean floor listening devices. The expected trade-off between economic resources to the coastal states for navigation rights for the naval and shipping states has surfaced in the text. The chief difficulty is the allocation of seabed resources, a fitting problem since it is the one which inspired Ambassador Pardo to initiate the talks in 1967.

However it takes shape, the new ocean order is bound to create some difficulties for naval operations. The old order was ideally suited for the mobility of powerful navies. The new order will impose restraints on ocean use where before there were none. The navies of the world will not only be called upon to respect new national, regional, and international maritime laws, but sometimes expected to help establish rules in times of conflict and uncertainty.

International society, like any society, needs a more complex legal system when more actors relate in more ways. The steadily increasing number of ocean users and uses means that a more detailed ocean law is inevitable. Navies will be ensnarled in this new complexity. But the new ocean order will not only impede the accomplishment of some naval missions, it will facilitate others. Remembrance and reverence of the old ocean order will not be enough. Navies must reexamine their relationships to the law of the sea and their preferences for legal rules keeping the emerging ocean order in mind.

Index

Index

Aden, Gulf of, 4
Ad Hoc Seabed Committee. *See* United
    Nations
Albania, 67
Algeria, 67
Arab-Israeli War of 1973, 5, 27
Arctic Sea, 4
Argentina, 63n
Atlantic Ocean, 4, 7, 25, 26, 27, 39, 40,
    41, 42, 46, 56, 59, 65
Australia, 8, 63n, 64
Austria, 64n, 69

Bab el Mandeb, Straits of, 3, 4
Bahamas, 64
Baltic Sea, 25, 26, 32
Belgium, 58, 64n, 69
Belize, 41
Bering Straits, 4
Black Sea, 25, 26, 32
Bolivia, 69
Brazil, 63, 63n
Brezhnev, L., 28
Britain. *See* Great Britain
Britain/Norway Gap, 25
Brown, G., 16
Bulgaria, 32, 33, 64n, 67
Burke, W., 75
Burma, 64n

Cambodia, 79
Canada, xv, 5, 8, 63n, 64, 66
Caribbean Sea, 4
carriers, aircraft and helicopter, 3, 24,
    41, 55, 63
Central Intelligence Agency, U.S., 11
Channel, English, 39, 40, 41
Chile, xiv, 63n, 64
China, 40, 63n, 66-67, 69
coast guard, 3, 40
coastal navy states, xvii, 63-74
coastal transit, 1, 7-8, 9, 10, 15, 16, 17,
    23, 26-27, 29, 33-34, 42, 44, 45,
    46-49, 55-56, 57-58, 58-59,
    68-70, 79-80, 82, 84-85, 90-91,
    91-92

Cod War of 1972-1973, 44, 77-79, 80,
    91
Cod War of 1975-1976, 44, 79
Colombia, 64n
Colombos, C.J., 4
Commerce and Arts, French Ministry
    of, 57
Commons, British House of, 41
Congo, 69
Congress, U.S., 10, 12-13, 16, 17-18
Congressional Research Service, U.S.,
    12
continental shelf, xiv, 12, 15, 29, 45,
    71, 72
conventional law of the sea, xiv-xv,
    xvii, 75-76, 80-85, 89, 91-92
Corfu Channel, 79
Cuba, 64n, 65-66
Cultural and Environmental Ministry,
    French, 57
customary law of the sea, xiv, xvii,
    75-80, 89, 91
Czechoslovakia, 32

Danish Straits, 25, 32-33, 65, 84
Dean, A., 13
Deaton, J., 25
Debré, M., 59
Defence, British Ministry of, 41, 43
Defense, French Ministry of, 53
Defense, U.S. Department of, 11, 12,
    13
Denmark, 25, 26, 64, 64n, 65
Disarmament, Conference on, 30, 71
dispute settlement, 85
Dominica, Straits of, 4
Dominican Republic, 64n
Dover, Straits of, 3, 4, 25

economic zones, 7, 16-17, 18, 26,
    33-34, 44-45, 47, 48, 59, 68-70,
    82, 84-85, 89, 91-92
Ecuador, xiv, 64n
Egypt, 64n
Eisenhower, D., 12
Ennals, D., 44, 46

environmental protection, 15, 17, 45,
46, 47, 48, 49, 66, 82, 83, 89, 90
Environmental Protection Agency,
U.S., 11
Environmental Quality, Council on,
U.S., 11
European Economic Community,
44-45, 58

Fabian Society, 45
Falkland Islands, 41
Faroe Islands, 26
Finland, 64, 64n
fishing, xiii, xiv, 13, 15, 16, 18, 28, 29,
31, 34, 40, 44-45, 46, 49, 58,
77-79, 80, 81, 82, 89, 90
Fisheries, Soviet Ministry of, 28-29
Ford, G., 18
Foreign Affairs, Soviet Ministry of, 28
Foreign Ministry, French, 57
Foreign Office, British, 43, 44
France, xiii, xvii, 40, 53-62, 63, 90-91
freedoms of the high seas, xiii-xiv,
9-10, 14, 27, 28, 29, 30, 39, 42,
44, 45, 46, 55, 56, 57, 58, 77,
79-80, 84, 89, 90, 91
French Navy. See France
French, S., 11

Geneva Conferences of 1958 and 1960.
See United Nations
Geneva Conventions of 1958, xiv, 4,
76
Geology, Soviet Ministry of, 28-29
Germany, East, 32, 33, 64n, 65
Germany, West, 58, 63n, 64
Ghana, 27, 67
Gibraltar, 41
Gibraltar, Straits of, 3, 5, 25, 26, 56, 65,
84
Gorshkov, S.G., 23, 24, 25, 27, 69
Great Britain, xiii, xvii, 8, 26, 27, 39-51.
53, 54, 55, 56, 57, 58, 59, 63, 65,
77-79, 80, 89, 90-91
Greece, 63n
Greenland, 26

Hague Conference of 1930, xiv
high seas. See freedoms of the high
seas
Hokkaido, 26
Hollick, A., 11
Hong Kong, 41
Hormuz, Straits of, 3, 4, 6, 65

Iceland, 26, 44, 49, 77-79
India, 63n, 70
Indian Ocean, 4, 5, 6, 7, 25, 26, 42, 46,
56, 66, 70
Indonesia, 5, 6, 64, 64n, 79
Indonesian Straits, 26, 79
Industry, French Ministry of, 57
innocent passage, 3-5, 7, 31, 32, 33, 47,
48, 65-68, 83, 84
intelligence, naval, 27, 41, 83
Inter-Agency Task Force on the Law
of the Sea, U.S., 11
Interior, U.S. Department of, 11, 12, 15
International Court of Justice, 77
International Law Commission. See
United Nations
Iran, 64n, 65
Iraq, 64
Israel, 5, 64, 79
Italy, 57, 63n

Jackling, R., 47
Japan, 4, 8, 26, 57, 63n, 64
Japan, Sea of, 4, 25, 26
Jeannel, R., 58, 59
Justice, U.S. Department of, 11

Keflavik Airbase, 78-79
Kennedy-Robeson Channels, 4
Kenya, 64
Khlestov, 31
Kolosovsky, I., 31, 33
Korean Straits, 26
Korea, South, 4, 26, 63n
Kulazhenkov, 34
Kuwait, 64, 67

La Perouse Strait, 26
Lebanon, 5

Lombok, Strait of, 5, 6
Libya, 64n, 71
Luns, 78-79

McDougal, M., 75
Mahan, A., 2, 68
Malacca, Straits of, 3, 5, 6, 84
Mali, 64n
Malta, xv, 33
Malaysia, 64, 64n, 65
Management and Budget, U.S. Office
    of, 11
manganese nodules, xv, 15, 29, 45
maritime trade. *See* merchant marine
Martinique, Straits of, 4
Mayaguez, 79-80
Mediterranean Sea, 5, 6, 7, 8, 18, 24, 25,
    26, 27, 41, 42, 46, 53, 55, 56, 59,
    66, 90
merchant marine, 10, 14, 15, 28, 31, 41,
    44, 45-46, 47-49, 56, 57-58, 65,
    66, 67, 77, 79-80, 81, 83, 90
Merchant Marine, Soviet Ministry of,
    28-29
Mexico, 63n
Mongolia, 65
Montreux, Convention of, 25-26
Moore, J.N., 11, 15
Morocco, 56, 64, 64n, 65
Morris, M., 11
Murmansk, 25

National Center for the Exploitation of
    the Oceans, French, 57
National Science Foundation, U.S., 11
National Security Council, U.S., 11
naval missions, xv-xvi, 1-10, 23-28,
    39-43, 53-56, 63, 67, 75
naval presence, xvi, 1, 2-3, 5, 8, 24, 25,
    27, 41, 54, 55, 69, 84
Netherlands, 58, 63n, 78
New Zealand, 64n
Nigeria, 64n, 67
Nixon, R., 12, 14, 15
North Atlantic Treaty Organization,
    26-27, 39, 40, 41, 42, 78-79
North Sea, 4, 8, 25, 27, 41, 45

Norway, 27, 64n
Norwegian Sea, 24
nuclear deterrence. *See* strategic deter-
    rence

oil and gas exploitation, xiii, 12, 15, 27,
    29, 40-41, 45, 46, 49, 89
Old Bahamas Channel, 4
Oman, 65, 67
Ombai-Wetar, Straits of, 5, 6
Oribe, 68-69, 70
Osgood, R., 4-5

Pacific Ocean, 6, 7, 25, 26, 46, 65
Pakistan, 64n
Paraguay, 64n
Pardo, A., xv, 33, 70-71, 92
Permanent Seabed Committee. *See*
    United Nations
Persian Gulf, 4, 6, 8, 46
Peru, xiv, 63n, 66, 68
Petropavlovsk, 25, 26
Philippines, 64, 64n
Poland, 32, 33, 64n
Politburo, Soviet, 28
pollution. *See* environmental protec-
    tion
Portugal, 13
projection of power ashore, 1, 2, 5, 7, 8,
    24, 39, 41

Red Sea, 4, 79
regional law of the sea, 90, 92
research, scientific, 8, 15, 17, 30, 46, 58,
    69-70, 81, 84, 92
Romanov, 34
Royal Navy. *See* Great Britain

Saint Lucia Channel, 4
Saint Vincent Passage, 4
Sanguinetti, A., 57
Sapozhnikov, 31
Schlesinger, A., 2
Science and Technology, Soviet State
    Committee on, 28-29
Scientific Research Institute of Mar-
    itime Transport, Soviet, 28

seabed, xv, 12, 15, 29, 34, 85, 92
Seabed Arms Control Treaty of 1971,
    9, 27, 35, 71
seabed, military use of, 1, 8-9, 10, 17,
    23, 27, 30, 34-35, 70-72, 82, 85,
    92
seabed, mining of, xiii, 12, 13, 15, 29,
    45, 46, 71, 81, 82, 92
sea control, 1, 2, 5, 8, 24, 40-41, 55
sea denial, 24, 25, 41
sea power, xiii, xvi, xvii, 2, 28, 49, 55,
    56, 59, 63, 64, 68-69, 76-80, 89,
    91
Seventh Fleet, U.S., 6
shipping. *See* merchant marine
Sixth Fleet, U.S., 5, 6, 8
South Africa, 64n
South China Sea, 5, 8
Soviet Navy. *See* Soviet Union
Soviet Union, xiii, xv, xvii, 3, 4, 6, 7, 8,
    9, 23-38, 40, 41, 42, 43, 44, 46,
    47, 48, 49, 53, 55, 56, 59, 63, 65,
    66, 67, 71, 72, 78, 81, 84, 85, 89,
    90-91
Spain, 6, 56, 63n, 64, 65, 67
Sri Lanka, 64n, 65, 66
SSBN, xiii, 1-2, 4-5, 8, 9, 23, 24, 40, 53,
    54, 55, 56, 63, 67, 71
State, U.S. Department of, 11, 12
Stevenson, J., 11, 14, 15, 16-17
straits passage, 1, 3-7, 9, 10, 14, 15, 16,
    17, 18, 23, 25-26, 27, 29, 31, 32,
    33, 42, 44, 45, 46-49, 56, 57-58,
    58-59, 64-68, 79, 82-84, 89, 90-91
strategic deterrence, xvi, 1-2, 5, 8,
    23-24, 39-40, 41, 42, 53-54, 55,
    63, 72
Suez Canal, 6, 25
Sunda Straits, 5, 6
Sweden, 25, 63n

Taiwan, 63n
Tanzania, 66
territorial seas, xiv, 7-8, 14, 17, 26-27,
    33, 39, 47, 55, 57, 58, 68-70, 84,
    85, 89

Thailand, 64n
Tiran, Strait of, 79
Tonga, 64
Trade, British Department of, 43
Transportation, U.S. Department of, 11
Treasury, U.S. Department of, 11, 12
Truman Proclamation, xiv
Tshushima, Straits of, 4
Tsugaru, Straits of, 26
Tuna Wars, xiv
Tunisia, 64n
Turkey, 25-26, 63n, 64
Turkish Straits, 25-26, 32-33, 84
Turner, S., 1, 69

Ukraine, 31, 32, 67
United Kingdom. *See* Great Britain
United Nations: Ad Hoc and Perma-
    nent Seabed Committees, xv, 14,
    30, 31, 33, 34, 68, 71, 80; Geneva
    Conference of 1958, xiv, 13, 31,
    33; Geneva Conference of 1960,
    xv, 33; International Law Com-
    mission, xiv; 1975 Geneva Ses-
    sion, xv, 80, 81, 82; 1974 Caracas
    Session, xv, 16, 17, 28, 31, 33, 43,
    44, 47, 58, 59, 65-67, 68, 69-70,
    80; 1976 New York Session, xv,
    80, 81, 84; Third Law of the Sea
    Conference, xvi, xvii, 18, 30, 44,
    46, 48, 59, 70, 75-76, 80-85, 89,
    91-92
United States, xiii, xiv, xv, xvii, 1-22,
    23, 24, 27, 29, 30, 33, 34, 41, 42,
    43, 44, 45, 46, 47, 48, 49, 53, 54,
    55, 56, 58, 59, 63, 66, 67, 71, 78,
    79-80, 81, 84, 85, 91
United States Navy. *See* United States
Uruguay, 64n, 68-69, 70

Venezuela, 63n
Vietnam, 13, 64n, 79

Warsaw Pact, 40
Western Chosen, Strait of, 4
Whitehall, 43, 45

Yellow Sea, 4
Yemen, 65, 67
Yemen, Democratic, 67
Yugoslavia, 64n

Zaire, 64
zones of peace, 65, 70
Zumwalt, E., 1

About the Author

Mark W. Janis is a graduate of Princeton where he received the A.B. degree in international relations. He was a Rhodes Scholar at Oxford, receiving the B.A. and the M.A. in jurisprudence. While an officer in the United States Naval Reserve he taught international law and relations for three years at the Naval Postgraduate School, Monterey, California. Mr. Janis was later a Research Associate of the Center for Advanced Research, Naval War College, Newport, Rhode Island. He is a member of the American Society of International Law and has clerked with law firms in New York and Chicago engaged in the practice of private international law. His published articles on the law of the sea have appeared in *Ocean Development and International Law, Naval Institute Proceedings, Naval War College Review,* the Occasional Papers of the Law of the Sea Institute, *Maritime Studies and Management,* and *San Diego Law Review.* He is presently a candidate for the J.D. degree at the Harvard Law School where he is Articles Editor of the *Harvard International Law Journal.*

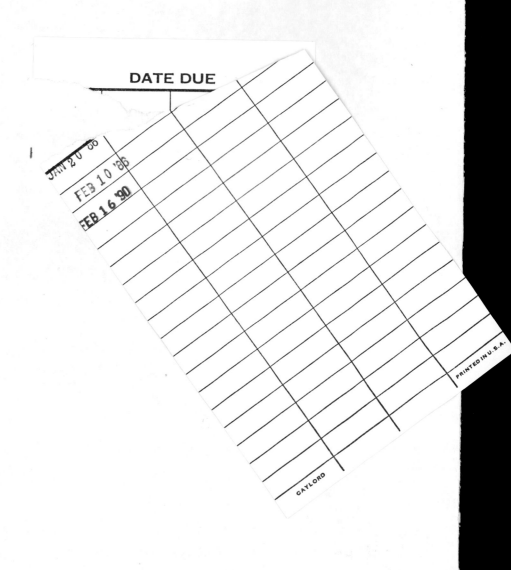

DATE DUE

JAN 20 '86

FEB 10 '86

FEB 16 '90

GAYLORD

PRINTED IN U.S.A.